#1 Amazon International Bestseller

GAPCULOGY

Bridging Cultural Gaps: How Modernization is Redefining Traditional Values Toward the Future.

DR. SID LIUFAU, MTC, HCC, CIT
Founder, Civility for All Foundation, Nevada, USA

GAPCULOGY: Bridging Cultural Gaps: How Modernization is Redefining Traditional Values Toward the Future.

ISBN: 978-978-60127-3-5

Scriptures quotations marked, unless otherwise indicated, are taken from the Holy Bible, the New International Version, and the New King James Version NKJV of the Holy Bible.

Dr. Sid Liufau's book titles may be purchased in bulk for educational, ministerial, business, fundraising, or sales promotional use. For information, please email- sidliufau.cfaf@gmail.com.

Printed in the United States of America

Published by

YPN
PUBLISHING & MEDIA

YPN Publishing and Media, LLC

Leading International Publishing and Media Group
30 N Gould Street, Sheridan, WY 82801 USA
3A/2B Kano Crescent Agbara Estate, LA, NG

Mobile: +2348023768604
Email: admin@ypnpublishers-media.com
Web: www.ypnpublishers-media.com
@ypnpublishers
@ypnpublishers
Ypnpublishingmedia

YPN Publishers & Media LLC
WhatsApp business account
Scan this code to start a WhatsApp chat with YPN Publishers & Media LLC.

DEDICATION

This book is dedicated to those navigating the intersections of tradition and modernity. To the teachers, leaders, and parents guiding the next generation, and to everyone seeking understanding across cultures—may this work inspire you to build bridges where walls once stood. To my family, whose support and love have made this journey possible.

ACKNOWLEDGMENT

I am grateful for God's plan of happiness.

I acknowledge the son of God, my Lord and Savior, Jesus Christ. He is the only reason I progress. I acknowledge my life's cultural mentors, Mother Sylvia Craig Tauati-Mata'ia, and my stepfather raised me. Samoan High Chief Fiamatai Tauati Matai'a Tagaloalangi.

My parents

I express my love and gratitude to all my siblings for my shaping and influence. And last, my undeniable eternal companion Sharene Teruya Liufau, who has been my advice, strength, and support. Our Afa-Kasi (mixed cultured children.) Ana, Sina, Tiare, Mevinga, and Teyvin-Justice.

My family

I Thank HRH Sir Dr. Clyde Rivers, Chancellor Michal Pitzl, and Vice Chancellor Ira Roach for their wonderful one-on-one mentorship regarding my philosophies.

I am inspired and thank Dr. Rozita Lee as co-founder of Civility for All Foundation, our nonprofit organization in Las Vegas, Nevada. I hope when I reach your fruitful age that I have half the love, wisdom, and nonstop energy to fight for humanity and civility for all.

Offering Global and Community Courses in Civility, Cultural Studies, and Health Communicational Wellness.
www.civilityforallfoundation.com.

I recognize my mentor and doer of good, HRH Sir Dr. Clyde River, the founder of the IChanged-Nations nonprofit organization.

I profoundly echo what I have learned under HRH Dr. Clyde Rivers and what I believe.

Driven by the constant change in generational civility and cultural mindsets, I am inspired to create a humanitarian platform of strength. This platform aims to address the resulting gaps in our generation and the next generation. Hence, I have coined the term "Gapculogy" to represent this concept and its meaning. In context, this word may benefit future Generational Cultural Gap misunderstandings.

I thank my lord and savior, Jesus Christ, whom I recognize is the fulfiller of all Gaps in our lives to allow mankind's progress through opposition in all things as an understanding that we are children of God who are here to succeed.

I am thankful for my family, my eternal companion, my children, and our culture of love, support, and civility. As a first-generation American citizen, I embrace this culture of civility of service in my life, family, and daily discourse that has given me a voice to educate, and uplift for the benefit of serving others, and in doing so, may we find joy and happiness.

In this book, I share my experiential truths of the good, the bad, and the ugly regarding my cultural experiences, evidence, and results from my non-progressive to progressive changes.

For this reason, I am an afa' kasi (mixed-blooded) Polynesian, Chinese, Scottish, and First-Generational American Citizen who shares my experiences as an American, and Polynesian, who believes in God and growing up with relatable influences of various cultures like many of you in America.

The point is whatever your race, ethnicity, or background may be, your sense of identity and cultural circumstances and struggles may be relatable.

My book is to help one understand how cultures play a huge part in our lives. I share and compare the good and the bad of cultural exchanges and confusion. At times, a feeling of loss, identity, and pride. There are countless full-blooded and mixed races of people with great cultures who did not grow up in their motherland but instead in an adopted land that they knew as home.

As a Hawaiian-born Samoan growing up in Orange County, California, I felt like I was in the 1982 fantasy movie 'Tron'. The plot is a futuristic virtual world of people taken from their real world and placed into a virtual world of a culture they only knew and lived.

The virtual world provides everything, but you still feel out-of-place knowing there is something else you were, but the virtual world you are in prevents you from denying anything else existed beyond the virtual world, confusing man's innate feeling.

My specific goal is to share whatever your cultural relations are through sharing my Polynesian cultural experiences. All cultures are relatable, so it is easy to understand. Most cultured people can be proud, loving, and family-orientated with their rich heritage. For me, multiple cultures such as being an American, a Christian, an Actor, a Stuntman, a Martial Artist, an Executive Protection, a Mobile DJ, or a Polynesian raised in a non-Polynesian land surrounded by different cultured perspectives.

Every facet of life's culture takes on a standard and understanding of its own. These cultural influences can cause clarity or confusion as to what your one cultured root really should be. Nothing good or bad learned is ever by mistake. It prepares and leads us to our next stage.

Respectfully Yours,

Dr. Sid Liufau, Senior MTC

5/2024

5/2017

5/1995

PREFACE

The seeds for "GAPCULOGY: Bridging Traditional Cultural Gaps; How Modernization is Redefining Traditional Values Toward the Future" were sown during countless conversations, observations, and personal reflections over the past several years. As I interacted with people from various backgrounds—each carrying their own unique traditional cultural narratives—it became increasingly clear that despite our diverse experiences, we were all navigating similar challenges brought on by rapid societal changes. These observations led me to ponder deeply about the traditional cultural shifts that not only define our past and present but will shape our future. This book is the culmination of that pondering—a comprehensive examination of how modernization impacts traditional values and the ways we can bridge the resulting gaps.

Throughout my career with the Civility For All Foundation, I have had the privilege of working with traveling to over 20 countries and communities around the world, advocating for civility and understanding across cultural divides. It was during these engagements that I realized the need for a deeper dialogue about the modern-day shifts occurring in our social fabric. The concept of "Gapculogy" emerged as a framework to address and study these changes, focusing on the intersection of multiple platforms, such as race, business, and religious cultures.

In this book, I invite readers to join me in exploring how each of these cultural dimensions is influenced by the forces of progress and modernization because it affects us all. Our journey will navigate through generational cultural misunderstandings, workplace cultural shifts, and the evolving roles of religion in public life, among other topics. Each chapter is designed to challenge assumptions and encourage a reflective approach to understanding the complexities of cultural evolution.

This preface serves as an invitation to open-mindedness and a call for engagement and understanding. As you turn these pages, I encourage you to reflect on your own experiences and consider how they intersect with the themes discussed. "GAPCULOGY" is not just a book; it is a starting point for conversations that are crucial in today's globalized changing society. For example, the American expression once used in our society "cash is king" was preferred, and suddenly, the COVID-19 pandemic hit and only plastic ATM cards or credit cards were accepted. Cash is out.

Let us embark on this journey with the hope that by understanding the generational gaps, we can find meaningful ways to bridge them, fostering a world where differences are not just tolerated but valued and understood. Together, through the study of Gapculogy, we can pave the way toward a future defined by deeper understanding and genuine civility for all is the result. Thank you for joining me in this important endeavor.

CONTENTS

INTRODUCTION

How can we bridge the cultural gaps that modernization has widened, ensuring that our cherished traditions evolve without losing their essence? As we stride into the future, can we maintain the continuity of our cultural heritage while embracing the inevitable changes brought about by technological advancement and global interconnectedness? How do we ensure that the wisdom of the past informs the progress of the present, fostering a society that values both tradition and innovation?

In this exploration, we delve into the intricate dynamics of evolving cultures in a world increasingly shaped by modernization and globalization. As you embark on this journey with me, we will uncover the profound changes impacting traditional cultural mindsets and examine how these transformations create gaps—but also bridges—between generations.

The concept of Gapculogy was borne from my desire to complement and expand upon the themes presented in my previous work, "Civility for All: Unleashing the Powers of Civility for the Next Generation." This book aims to deepen our understanding of how cultural shifts affect not only personal interactions but also societal norms across various dimensions—race, business, and religion.

As we move through the chapters, we will confront the reality that the cultural foundations we have long considered stable are, in fact, in flux. This fluidity can lead to misunderstandings and conflicts, as different generations interpret core values through diverse lenses. However, it also presents a unique opportunity to redefine these values in ways that are inclusive and forward-thinking.

Throughout "GAPCULOGY," we will explore specific cultural arenas—Generational Cultures, Work Culture, Religious Cultures, Interculture, and Intraculture—each reshaped by the forces of change. These explorations are not just academic; they are deeply personal. They reflect a journey of growth and understanding, as both our experiences and our environments continually influence each of us.

By the end of this book, I hope you will not only have a greater understanding of the cultural gaps that exist in our modern world, but also be equipped with the knowledge to bridge these gaps. Through stories, research, and personal insights, we will learn how to engage with our world's evolving cultural landscape, not with fear or apprehension, but with openness and civility.

Let us begin this important conversation, and together, explore how we can keep peace in the public square by embracing change and celebrating diversity. Join me in uncovering the essence of Gapculogy, and let's redefine what it means to live and interact in a world rich with varied and evolving cultural identities.

Dr. Sid Liufau, *MTC, HCC, CIT*

I am a Civility Ambassador for Generational Differences

- My soul overflows with love and reproving tools.
- My mind quickens to empathy and justice.
- I have equipped my ears to listen to learn, then learn to listen to the equilibrium of balance.
- The Communicational Generational table setter for the voiceless to be heard.

My callings embody the Lord Omnipotent's commandment; to love one another and treat one another fairly. As a Civility Ambassador, I will empower others by teaching civility tools that help those who are negatively affected, disconnected, divided, angered, contentious, hostel, and noncompliant towards others and themselves. Including communication health solutions.

Using the tools can empower one to have a voice and to be heard. The hope is to allow others in conflict to hear your truths. So, a resolution of data can be offered that results in the goal, allowing for peace in the public square.

As a family man of faith and a leader in my Pacific Island communities and mainstream communities, I have been part of multiple community nonprofit organizations aimed at helping and supporting our communities.

The takeaway is those issues that arise in our communities can swiftly become a setback because of the lack of resources and tools when in the ditches of non-progression.

Civility Foundation that focuses on Communication Health is worth the best day of celebration when issues are resolved and it is the reason I stand tall, proud, and grateful for having learned HRH Sir Dr. Clyde Rivers' affective tools and combined with my findings to combat all generations of error mindsets and offering solutions.

Accepting the challenge presented by HRH Sir Dr. Clyde Rivers, I was introduced to Chancellor Michal Pitzl and Vice Chancellor Ira Roach. After delivering my civility speech to the graduates, they approached me to discuss the message I had conveyed.

Dr. Rivers also shared that Chancellor Pitzl created a platform known as Searchademics. As explained, Searchademics can search words in the dictionary platform and, if it is not a processed word, she can also use

Searchademics to create new words along with the definition and add them to the dictionary.

This is huge. It never crossed my mind that I would be considered for this platform, but Dr. Rivers shared a very moving thought. He stated that I have a gift and a way of expressing this gift that gets people to listen. Dr. Rivers extended an invitation to me to present a new word and definition to be considered a modern-day philosopher.

Although this sounds fascinating, of course, this is not an easy process. As a matter of fact, it seemed almost impossible, then it hit me with my experiential truth. I will find a cultured word and universally apply its definition on multiple generational levels.

I do not know whether they will use this specific word and attached definition or not, however, for what it is worth, I enjoyed the challenge. I had to go before a board of professors to present live my dissertation and answer questions.

Now that this book is out again, I do not know whether the board of philosophy professors will accept this word and definition.

Allow me to explain the title of this book **Gapculogy**.

My intention was to write a book that complements and provides a deeper comprehension of Civility for All: Unleashing the Powers of Civility for the Next Generation.

I considered my perspectives and how I arrived at my thoughts. I also understand that everyone depending on where you are at in life has concluded with your perspective. And as to one's perspective, it may and continues to change as we continue to learn and grow in life.

My prayer is that the insights I provide can be of value to anyone in need of change or seeking guidance on an unexplored journey.

1

2

3

4

1 Dr. Sid Liufau Co-Founder of Civility for All Foundation.

2 HRH Sir Dr. Clyde Rivers Founder of I Change Nations Foundation

3 Chancellor Michal Pitzl of UGCSI and Searchademics

4 Vice Chancellor Ira Roach Founder Pastors Civility

In all things, everything is relative and relatable.

When I considered Gapculogy, it opened countless doors to specific titles of perspectives I listed.

- Generational Cultures
- Work Culture
- Religious Cultures
- Interculture Cultures
- Intraculture Cultures

All these various cultures are constantly changing and bringing differences that cause generational Gaps presenting issues in people's views of truth.

Creating Civility in a nutshell and fostering facts does not mean we should agree or that we will agree.

As a matter of fact, NOT agreeing with someone else's truth is OK. I define the word 'OK' as "Opened Knowledge." This means your experiences determine your truth.

My experiences determine my truth. It's OK to have opposing views, only if we do it peacefully. Civility's main goal is to "Keep Peace in the Public Square." Now Let's get back to Basics.

"

In 'GAPCULOGY,' the confluence of tradition and modernity becomes a powerful force for cultural evolution, redefining values for the generations to come." — Dr. Sid Liufau

Chapter 1

CIVILITY FOUNDATIONS AND COMPONENTS

The basics of fostering a platform and exhibiting polite and respectful behavior in social interactions is the overall goal of keeping peace and order in the public square.

The fostering platforms create a two-edged sword perspective. I will note in every chapter and every opportunity that relates to civil positive behavior, attributes, and belief that when they are not being utilized, compared to a seed planted in our minds, can create the opposite effect which is a negative view that will be the results most likely seen and felt.

Individuals tend to have a positive response to receiving good and courteous treatment. An approach centered on civility regarding intrapersonal, interpersonal relationships, and intrancompassing elements such as politeness, etiquette, and kindness for both current and future generations holds value; however, several inquiries warrant further investigation.

Although most individuals engage in civil interactions with one another regularly, anyone can experience occasional lapses of the opposite behavior through negative experiences, upbringing, drugs, alcohol, or just rotten to the unsympathetic core people.

Upon closer examination of the various dimensions of civility, it becomes evident that there is a wealth of knowledge to be gained regarding the origins of incivility and the negative tactics that can be implemented to cultivate civil conduct, even in situations of potential hazard.

In my belief, through experiences, there must be opposition to all things. This understanding of potential hazards, whether through personal or public outcomes, is certainly clear in specific negative situations such as extreme protests.

However, let me be clear, the negative situation is not the concern and or the worries. The concern arises from our inherent willingness as human beings to act and seek resolutions.

We should already have a figured out or have a planned response to having a solid foundation already prepared, not be swayed, forced, or coerced through pressure.

Example: I go to the store to do my food shopping for my family. After spending time shopping, I now have a cart full of items and food. Now checking out at the cash register, I learn the store does not accept cash. They only accept ATM cards. I only have cash. My question to you is, what is your next response?

Most of the time as human beings when we are inconvenienced, negativity is our response.

However, if we have already set a foundation such as civility of understanding, then we will work through the negativity as we would in positive situations to find solutions.

First, understanding that those workers do not make corporate decisions, so perspective is huge. The expression is 'do not shoot the messenger.'

What does that mean? Do not put the blame where it does not belong or where it cannot change the underlying issue.

> ***"People generally respond well to courteous treatment, and an emphasis on civility, politeness, etiquette, and kindness benefits both current and future generations.***

Did you know, in comparison, that the opposite of civility (Incivility) causes loss of business and loss of revenue?

Christine Porath, a management researcher explains to understand what incivility is and how it affects others negatively.

What is Incivility? When people foster incivility, it is a negative attribute such as disrespect, condescension, rudeness, or insensitivity.

It includes a lot of negative behaviors as well ...

- Mocking or belittling someone
- Teasing people in ways that sting
- Offensive jokes
- Interrupting meetings or being dismissive

The company CPM launched studies and surveys on performance and the bottom line: Sent a survey to business school alumni working in all different organizations. They were asked to write a few sentences about one experience where they were treated rudely, disrespected, or encountered insensitivity.

One person talked about a boss who made insulting statements like "That is kindergarten work."

- A supervisor who threatens certain coworkers with the insubordination of not following work policy but looks the other way when the same is done by those who are close to him.

- Another tore up someone's work in front of the entire team.
- A coworker who continually discriminates, and it is overlooked by the boss.

What we found is that incivility made people less motivated to put themselves out there for the company.

Incivility made people less motivated and due to not being corrected, cost the company money.

- 66% cut back their work efforts, asking why they would put themselves out there to only be smashed.
- 80% lost work time worrying, continually venting, and spreading negativity.
- 12% left their job, with the mindset that 'I will find another job that has my best interest.'

The powerhouse technology company Cisco read about the incivility survey and carried out one. Afterward, they found out that incivility in their workplace was estimated to cost them conservatively 12 million dollars a year.

What if you're not the one experiencing incivility? What if you just see it or hear it?

Another study tested peers' insulting a group member.

- What was found is that witness performances decreased too. Not just marginally but significantly 25% & 45%.

Incivility is a biting bug. It's contagious and we become carriers of it simply by being around it. If Incivility causes an enormous cost, why do we still see so much of it?

The number one reason people leave a job is financially correlated; it is not worth it.

The second reason, and more terminal is because of stress.

- People feel overwhelmed.
- People vent when they feel pure pressure or feel they have no control.
- People will not vent their concerns because they feel they will appear less leader-like in front of peers.
- People wonder: Do nice guys finish last? The data does show that nice guys don't finish last.

November 2023, on an airplane flight, a female passenger stated that she was told to wait in her seat as other passengers were already in line waiting. As people often do on a flight, they wait in their seats until they must go to the restroom. Her reaction, not being able to wait, was to stand up, pull down her tights, squat, and pee in the aisleway in front of other passengers. She said she could not wait.

The question for ourselves regarding this result is, is this a negative result? In a society of order, it will be taken as disrespectful and shameful by most passengers. To the individual who is forced to wait but needs to use the toilet and yet can no longer hold it, do what they must.

I can recall an experience that took place in my mid-teens. I had an uncle who moved into our home. Once he got comfortable, he forced me and my siblings to practice self-defense martial arts. Without having a choice to do so and after years of training in martial arts of self-defense, I saw outcomes of following this pattern. I hated the method my uncle used to force us to train. Although learning how to fight and protect us was a pattern of force.

Mean, rude, and blunt, his bullying pattern took its toll. One day in the living room, he spoke to me in Samoan. I did not understand the language. My mom sitting nearby translated, "Go pour uncle a cup of orange tea." I walked to the kitchen and on the stove, I poured out of the cattle this freshly brewed tea. I returned to my uncle and handed him the cup of tea. He looked in the cup and gave me an angry stare. He told me to return and put tea leaves in the cup. I had never done this before for anyone. So, I returned to the cattle, emptied the tea back into the pot, filled it with tea leaves, and gave it to him. All I could remember was flying out the front porch door after being punched. I landed flat on my back with a bleeding, broken nose.

What did I learn from that incident? I learned that I was incompetent, unloved, and someone who deserved to be bullied and beaten down.

Later in life, I learned my uncle was a bully. I learned that as a kid, his father and grandfather beat him down.

The Danger of Screaming or Bullying

Preparation for an infant or child. I witnessed an experiment of the reaction of an infant or young child sitting in the lap of his mother. The child was given a small toy box with a loose LED top that when removed, held a small toy in the box. The experimental instructor talked to the child with a low pleasant voice and the infant seemed to follow the instruction. He played with the box, removed the top, and pulled out the toy. His facial expressions showed he was enjoying himself. His brain function and motor skills were being stimulated. After a few minutes, the box and toy were removed from the child's table.

Next experiment; a lady walked into the room holding a newspaper. She stood to the right of the child at the end of the table. She began yelling at the news. The yelling causes confusion and fear. The child's facial expression said it all: fear!

The lady stopped yelling. The experimental person put the box and toy on the table and asked the child to place the toy back in the box, giving the child twenty seconds to do so. As the lady yelled, the child shifted his gaze and became fixated on the toy, frozen. This experiment shows that when violence is used on innocent minds such as infants, teens, and immature adults, it hinders their progression. STOP USING VIOLENT EDUCATION to raise infants, children, teens, and others.

As an adult, I made sure my kids understood they do not bully others or allow anyone to bully them. I hate it when anyone gets bullied. In my mom's generation, bullying was a way of life being abused. Maybe it was commonplace back then, but not in the year 2000s.

Generational Differences

In mid-September 2023, I went to a TGFI restaurant with eight of my civility Dr. friends to have a dinner. The waitress given the task to serve our table was probably in her early twenties. She was of the 'Gen-Z' generation. The issue our older generation had was that this young waitress reached across one of us to serve someone else food or drinks. By the facial expression of my 90-year-old Dr. friend, when the waitress continued to reach in front of her to serve someone else, it was like the end of the world had come. Sadly, I think the 'Gen-Z' server had no clue that she was offending us by reaching across one person to serve another.

However, my friend is a passivist; one who does not want to make a big deal. So she hesitated to tell her friends about what was bothering her. I cannot blame the 'Gen-Z' waitress if she is doing something she does not consider offensive towards someone else, especially when those feeling offended say nothing. How would an offender be aware of his or her offence unless he or she is told?

Six Better Ways to Disagree

by President Russel M Nelson

- Express feelings with love.
- Don't rigorously defend your position.
- Don't think you know best.
- Let the spirit guide your conversation.
- Don't compete.
- Be filled with charity, the pure love of Christ.

Those that appear more civil are twice as likely to be viewed as leaders and they perform higher by 13%.

Being Civil Pays

- Because people see you as an important and powerful unique combination of two key characteristics.

Two-Key Characteristics

- Warm and friendly. Caring.
- Competent and Smart. Follow Policies Correctly.

So where do you start?

How can you lift another and make people feel respected?

The nice thing is that it does not require a huge shift.

Small things can make a difference

- Thanking people, giving people credit
- Listening attentively, humbly asking questions
- Being polite, acknowledging others
- and smiling has an impact.

Research studies show that we are more productive, creative, helpful, happy, and healthy.

Each one of us can be better

- We can lift others around us, at work, online, at home, in schools, in our communities, and at home.
- In every action, think about who you want to be.
- Don't be argumentative; Do you want to be right, or do you want to be happy?

Follow the Civility Two Pillar Rule

- Golden Rule: Treat Others like you want to be treated.
- Golden Question: If the shoe were on the other foot, would the decision you make be different?
- Treat others not necessarily as they are but as they can become.

Parents, grandparents, and guardians, why do we change our mindset for others, regarding what we do for our children?

We try to do everything for our children so they can learn and grow. We know once they start to learn; we know we can build a foundation where we can trust them to understand where we are coming from.

Why do we not have the same perspective towards wanting to educate others whom we bump heads with regarding their different perspective of view?

I love the example of truth taught through a learned perspective. When I read this article, it not only made sense but is evidence of the truth today in progressing together, not just as individuals, family members, a community, a nation, but most importantly as to the survival of human beings.

Humanity Rule of Civilization

Years ago, a student asked Anthropologist Margret Mead what she considered to be the first sign of civilization in a culture. The student expected Mead to talk about fishhooks, clay pots, or grinding stones.

But no. Mead said that the first sign of civilization in an ancient culture was a femur (thigh bone) that had been broken and then healed. Mead explained that in the animal kingdom, if you break a leg, you die. You cannot run from danger, go to the river for a drink, or hunt for food. You are meant for prowling beasts. No animal survives a broken leg long enough for the bone to heal. A broken femur that has healed is evidence that someone has taken the time to stay with the one that fell, has bound up the wound, has carried the person to safety, and has tended the person through recovery. Helping someone else through difficulty is where civilization starts, Mead said."

We are at our best when we are civil and serving others. Let me clearly stipulate in my choosing these words the difference that the term 'serving' differs in meaning to someone in need and someone wanting help. Some are unwilling to do for themselves and are unable or cannot do for themselves. Jesus taught not to give someone fish, but rather to teach them to fish.

This chapter presents the Five Building Blocks of Cultural Civility intended for the imminent generations.

The following discourse expounds upon the quintessential principles of cultural understanding using the foundations of civility that are deemed imperative for the forthcoming generations based on the past and present generations.

Chapter 2

BUILDING BLOCKS OF NEXT-GEN CULTURE AND GENERATIONAL GAPS

The Five Building Blocks of Culture Generational Gapculogy for the Next Generation

- What is the History and Origin of the Polynesian People?
- What is Gapculogy?
- Polynesian Culture of love and respect.
- Exhibit a sense of responsibility by demonstrating a sense of accountability and reliability in your actions and decisions.
- Future Cultural Perspectives.

The Five Building Blocks of Civility for the Next Generation

- What is the History and Origin,

- First, this is specifically talking about INTRA cultures. There are specific cultures I will point out.
- Race Ethnicity Cultures
- Business and Work Cultures
- Religious / Law Enforcement / Military Cultures

However, for this first leg, I will focus on the Intra-race and ethnicity of ALL cultures. However, as an example, I will use and reference my Polynesian Culture.

In the beginning my introduction, as a reminder, I used an analogy which I surmised as to not blame the messenger who is not responsible and cannot change policies in the workplace. That said, I note regarding change; I use the new (AI) artificial intelligence platform to summarize my Polynesian island history and origins. Anything with an asterisk (*) shows the information provided by (AI) summary.

Polynesians

*Polynesians are a group of closely related people who are native to Polynesia, an expansive region of Oceania in the Pacific Ocean.

*One theory of archaeological discovery shares that their influential roots can trace early prehistoric origins to Island Southeast Asia and form part of the larger Austronesian ethnolinguistic group with an Urheimat in Taiwan[1]. Tracing Polynesian languages places their prehistoric origins in Island Melanesia, Maritime Southeast Asia, and ultimately, in Taiwan[2].

The first settlers of the Pacific islands of Tonga and Vanuatu likely arrived from Taiwan and the northern Philippines between 2,300 and 3,100 years ago[1]. Once they had reached the mid-ocean archipelagos of Fiji, Tonga, and Samoa, these seafarers were alone in the ocean, for only they had the canoes and navigational skills needed to push so far into the Pacific[1].

*Polynesian culture is the culture of the indigenous peoples of Polynesia who share common traits in language, customs, and society. The development of Polynesian culture is typically divided into four different historical eras: Exploration and settlement (c. 1800 BC—c. AD 700) Development in isolation (c. 700—1595) [3].

*Polynesian navigation of the Pacific Ocean and its settlement began thousands of years ago. The inhabitants of the Pacific islands had been voyaging across vast expanses of ocean water sailing in double canoes or outriggers, using nothing more than their knowledge of the stars and observations of sea and wind patterns to guide them.

*Skilled navigators in double-hulled canoes gradually discovered remote islands to the east, using their knowledge of the stars and the winds to return home safely1.

The prevailing European view was that any migration resulted from accidental storms or current drifts, not purposeful indigenous navigation**2.** The early voyagers worked their way eastward from the Asian side of the Pacific, moving from island to island by exploiting seasonal westerly wind reversals3.

Another theory with influential shared evidence is that Polynesians migrated from an origin in the Pacific known as Havai'ki.

The source of life of Hawaiki history is known as a place of great importance in the Maori tradition and appears in many Maori songs, proverbs, and whakapapa (genealogies). In tradition, the seas in their canoes.

The source of life. Hawaiki is the place from which humans are born, and to which they go after death–it is strongly associated with the cycle of birth, life, and death. Hawaiki represents all that is good and powerful. It is a mystical place where people turn into birds or descend into the underworld.

Home of the Gods

In some traditions, the supreme being IO created Hawaiki. The gods are believed to live there, including the trickster demigod Maui, whose deeds are famous throughout Polynesia. The first woman, Hineahuone, was fashioned from the soil of Hawaiki.

> *When faced with an inconvenience, such as a store not accepting cash, a foundation of civility helps us respond positively and work towards a solution, recognizing that frontline workers are not responsible for corporate policies.*

Location Unknown

Marori and Pakeha alike have wondered about the true location of Hawaiki. The actual location has never been confirmed, and it is uncertain if it is a real physical island or a mythical place.

Some have associated Hawaiki with the Tahitian islands' art (Rangiatea, in Maori). Like Hawaiki, Rangiata is seen as both a physical and spiritual place.

Some people thought that Maori might have originated from Polynesia, India, or even Mesoptamia. More recent scholars have admitted it is difficult to decide on the 'true' location of a place that is also mythological.

Another possible theory is the beliefs and practices of the indigenous people of the ethnogeographic group of Pacific islands known as Polynesia (from Greek *poly* 'many' and *nēsoi* 'islands').

Polynesia encompasses a huge triangular area of the east-central Pacific Ocean. The triangle has its apex at the Hawaiian Island in the north and its base angles at New Zealand (Aotearoa) in the west and Easter Island (Rapa Nui) in the east. It also includes (from northwest to southeast) Tuvalu, Tokelau, Wallis and Futuna, Samoa (formally Western Samoa), Tonga, Niue, the Cook Islands, and French Polynesia. (Tahiti and Society Islands, Marquesas Islands, the Austral Islands, and the Tuamotu Acrchipelago, including the Gambier Islands (formally the Managareva Islands) and Pitcairn Island. At the turn of the 21st century, about 70 percent of the total population of Polynesia lived in Hawaii.

The physical environment of the Polynesian islands is not as favorable for human habitation as it might at first seem. It certainly presented difficulties when the ancestors of the Polynesians entered the area some 2,000 to 3,000 years ago, first settling on the western islands—Wallis and Futuna, Samoa, and Tonga—which were devoid of much that was needed for human habitation.

As a result, early people had to take in a wide variety of subsistence items, including most of the useful plants and all the domestic animals they required. The physical environment has continued to exert a marked influence on Polynesian culture.

Western colonialism has radically altered Polynesian cultures. European explorers navigated much of the area in the latter quarter of the 18th century, and the first missionaries arrived in the late 1700s and early 1800s.

Britain annexed New Zealand through the Treaty of Waitangi (1840), but interethnic tension arose between the indigenous Maori. Other colonial powers that laid claim to various parts of Polynesia included France, Germany, New Zealand, the United States, and Chile.

But for me, the takeaway is an article found in the Time Magazine under **Archaeology of Samoa** that began with the first systematic survey of archaeological remains on Savai'i island by Jack Golson in 1957.[1] Since then, surveys and studies in the rest of Samoa have uncovered major findings of settlements, stone and earth mounds including star mounds, Lapita pottery remains, and pre-historic artifacts.[2]

An important part of archaeology in Samoa and Oceania involves finding the answer to the origins of Polynesians,[3] ongoing research which is being undertaken in conjunction with other fields, including linguistics and genetics.

The oldest date so far from pre-historic remains in Samoa has been *calculated* by New Zealand scientists to a likely true age of circa 3,000 BP (Before Present) from a Lapita site at Mulifanua during the 1970s.[4]

What is Gapculogy?

Gapculogy is based on a traditional cultural mindset that is constantly changing because of modernization and progression resulting in Gaps (changes) towards the next generations.

Relatable cultural influences are acknowledged in all generations. However, there are multiple identities of cultures. For example, here are three that I refer to specifically when I speak of cultures.

1. Race Cultures.
2. Business Cultures.
3. Religious Cultures.

Any group with a traditional culture is affected by the involving relevance of change due to modernization and progression, resulting in gaps.

Case and point: Polynesian cultures are ethnic race cultures that are governed by traditions, languages, cultural dress, foods, songs, dance, etc.

The great thing about the Polynesian cultures is that they are considered by comparison in America as the minority of minorities ethnicity race cultures. Each Polynesian ethnicity within the Polynesian construct of islands that include Hawaii, Samoa, Tonga, Tahiti, New Zealand, Cook Islands, etc. Each island has its specific cultural traditions, chiefs, identity, language, tapestries, foods, costumes, dress, jewelry, and protocols.

The upbringing of people in all cultures is normally considered traditional, taught to the next cultural generation, and passed down from generation to generation.

All cultures have their pros and cons. Most cultures live the Civility foundations that include love, respect, compassion, and respect. These foundations are strong pillars that, if embraced, will enable both the people and their culture to thrive.

However, cultures are constantly changing because of the modernization influences of their existential timeline.

Each lineage is influenced by what is relevant and, if affected, must adjust to find to adapt the new changes yet continue to keep their past cultures relevant, alive, and strong.

> ***All cultures have their pros and cons. Most cultures live the Civility foundations that include love, respect, compassion, and respect. These foundations are strong pillars that, if embraced, will enable both the people and their culture to thrive.***

Case and Point

Polynesian cultural changes on the island are not as extreme as changes off the island, especially for the millennial, Gen-Z, and Alpha generations whose parents have constantly raised their children in the Polynesian culture, however, slated with adapted the country's culture they live in.

I recall my visit to Bankok Thailand to work on a film. During my day off, I went to watch a movie in a Thai movie theater. As a Samoan and American citizen, used to our movie culture of relaxation, popcorn, and soda.

I was not ready for the Thai culture movie theater. Before the movie is shown, the president comes on screen and everyone in the Thai national anthem plays. I recall sitting in the front row watching the screen.

Suddenly, I heard something small and near where I was sitting. I turned around to see who threw it and, to my shock, everyone in the theater was standing during the Thai national anthem.

I had no clue this was their culture. It was told to me that anyone sitting down in the movie theater during their national anthem is a sign of disrespect.

All cultures of our great-great-grandparents, grandparents of parents' family, and loved ones who ever lived indeed had to adjust to their generation to keep the cultural ethnicity foundation alive.

Culture Clash

When cultures are in the midst of traditional mindset changes regardless of the issues or circumstances, the changes will never be easy to accept by a generation that has been living the foundation for decades and even centuries. Such as the case of the following influences of worn, torn war.

Cause and Effect

October 2022, Dr. Clyde Rivers, alongside other ICN and Civility Ambassadors who were invited to Birmingham, United Kingdom, shared their experiences. UK mayors invited HRH Dr. Rivers to talk with UK law enforcement leadership regarding the unfolding crisis.

The in-charge UK government had been working to help the Ukrainian cultured refugees, and Afghan cultured refugees all seemed to have made a hasty exit because of the war from their countries seeking shelter in the United Kingdom.

However, months after the UK accepted these specific Ukraine and Afghan cultures to live the accepted intra-UK country's culture. Sadly, the two cultures seemed to be treated differently regarding living conditions and expectations.

The Ukrainians received better treatment compared to the Afghan people. In any humanitarian point of view of fairness, any type of discriminating action against any culture can and will cause an upheaval by people who seek fair treatment and conditions.

After Dr. Rivers' 12-day visit, he returned home, and a few months later; we met in Las Vegas. I recall Dr. Rivers stating how the UK mentality seemed to still live some 50 years back in the past. Dr. Rivers shared that he had walked away understanding that the UK leadership had failed to provide fair treatment to Afghan refugees like they did to the Ukrainian refugees.

In short, Dr. Rivers shared there was a lack of civility towards darker skin color. Division towards the Afghan refugees seems to arise from the cultural sensitivity surrounding their conditions. The two different worlds of cultures, yet one was kept in the hotels to live in, which was supposed to be a temporary fix.

The UK leadership culture seemed oblivious and unaware of how these other cultures functioned and how to deal with the specific expectations. It continued sharing that darker-skinned people seem to still be treated second rate less than white people. So, when an uprising by the people's notable feelings is denied and ignored, then eventually the outcome of people lashing out negatively should not be a surprise to those leaders.

Dr. Rivers shared that if the UK leadership mentality does not change this situation, most likely it will end in a negative eruption like most eruptions that denied humanitarian and cultural treatment.

My immediate thoughts were if the UK leadership would accept the Afghans and the Ukrainians due to the humanitarian conditions away from war. And yet provide areas of culture only to provide two different outcomes than the hosting nation should have thought this through.

I believe we can provide civility training seminars on Gapculogy cultural and generational recognition to clearly understand cultural compliance that includes the hosting nation's laws, culture and foundations agreed to educate the UK culture before accepting these nations.

Political reporter Becky Morton

Today August 2023, Many Afghan refugees have been "let down" by the UK, with some living in hotels for up to two years and now facing eviction, a think tank has said.

More in common said lessons needed to be learned so future refugees were better supported.

It comes on the anniversary of the UK's evacuation programmed and the fall of Kabul to the Taliban on 15 August 2021. Minister Johnny Mercer admitted there had been "challenges" but said he was determined to make Afghan schemes work.

Operation Pitting saw the UK airlift around 15,000 people out of Kabul - including British nationals, as well as people who worked with the UK in Afghanistan and their family members.

The authorities placed those who had nowhere to live in government-funded hotels. This was supposed to be temporary accommodation, but by the end of March, there were still around 8,800 Afghans living in hotels.

The government has imposed a deadline at the end of August for Afghans to be moved out of hotels in September 2023, but **councils have warned some are facing homelessness as they cannot find anywhere else to live**.

More in Common, an organization founded in the murder wake of Labor MP Jo Cox, surveyed 132 Afghans in the UK.

It told of failures in communication with local authorities and the Home Office on housing, rental applications being repeatedly rejected, and unsuitable homes being offered, sometimes hundreds of miles away.

One example saw a refugee living in temporary accommodation in Bristol, where they had family, offered permanent housing in Northern Ireland.

Hawaii, Priced out of Paradise

For far too long, Hawaii's ridiculous uptick in Intra-US taxes has been noted as an underline failed system that has caused issues long ago following the overthrow of the sovereign nation of Hawaii. The unjust demands of providing a no-win scenario for the locals residing and especially for the Kanaka-Maoli the native Hawaiians.

The occupying USA nation seemingly confiscated the Hawaiian island land grab to set up this no-win limited provision for the indigenous Hawaiian people who must wait on a list provided by the US governments to be recognized by the US racial requirements for land to be owned by Hawaiian and must provide proof of blood percentage.

This Intra-US government requirement has been aspirated by racist tone to the generations of Hawaiians who marry into other mixed races. Now, regardless of the land being allowed to be given to Hawaiian families, this US state mandates the native Hawaiian family member now to have a higher percentage of Hawaiian bloodline.

If the Hawaiian family members do not meet the requirement, then the state of Hawaii government will not turn over land to the hapa (half) mixed Hawaiians who are not the required Hawaiian percent by blood.

To understand why Lahaina Maui is important to any Hawaiian, Kanaka Maoli is to understand the first King Kameahamea Hawaiian History.

President William McKinley Annexed the Republic of Hawaii

McKinley reversed the policy of his predecessor, Grover Cleveland, and advocated for Hawaii to become a US territory. After the Spanish-

American War, the strategic importance of the islands' location in the Pacific Ocean became more apparent, and an annexation resolution supported by McKinley passed the House and Senate in 1898. The episode marked an end to a lengthy battle between native Hawaiians and white American businessmen for control of the local government. The last monarch of Hawaii, Queen Lili'uokalani, was overthrown in 1893, and Benjamin Harrison sent a bill to the Senate to approve the annexation. But Grover Cleveland became president before it was passed, and he withdrew the bill. When McKinley became president, he tried to reintroduce the bill but was stymied by the Hawaiian Patriotic League, who kept the US at bay until the events of 1898.

Hawaiians' history tells a differently different history that is not the same as the United States claims that includes the act of congress, President William Mikinley agreed to annex Hawaii and Queen Lili'uokalani who did not have a choice for Hawaii to be annexed as the Fifth State.

Hawaii's Queen Lili'uokalani was dealing with American and Canadian businessmen who were permitted by the Queen to start a commodity export business. Yet the businessmen demanded more land and opportunities. Instead, the Queen declared the end of their agreement. These businessmen hired strong-armed men to kill Hawaiians who stood in the way.

The Queen then saw the position she was in and flew to Washington DC to speak before Congress and pleaded for the US to interfere with the threats from these tyrannical greedy businessmen who were now raping the Hawaiian natural commodities and resources.

The United States sent their Navy to intervene with the militia threats and the rest was history. The Queen was placed under house arrest and Hawaii with no choice.

Native Hawaiian history teaches that Hawaii's reigning Queen Lili'uokalani was held prisoner under palace arrest by the United States military with the scenario of threats on the Hawaiian people if she did not cooperate.

The contributing factors for the US government were their greed factors. Their pretentious care was to protect the people, instead it was the commodities, minerals, the land, and most importantly how Hawaii could serve as the strategic military point against any nation attacks from the Pacific seas.

Outraged: A repeat of Hawaiians once again on descendants of the Alii's and their posterity threaten, dead, and given no voice to speak.

I work in a community where the motto is 'See Something, Say Something'. The world needs to wake up! When the currency of common people is worthless to the people who have been forcing their ways of life on others. It is time to Stand Up, Speak Out, and act accordingly. For far too long, political injustice has been choking the people with taxes and inflation, pricing us out.

As a Hawaii-born baby, if I were to make an exact comparison of what I can compare to what Hawaii has already undergone, I would say this is the same course of evil, greedy underhanded agenda that the US government and the 1% have intentional attacks the residents of Lahaina and the sovereign nation of the Hawaiian people.

Suspicious Acts of Fire, Death, and Coincidences

August 12, 2023, such is the case in Lahaina, Maui of the Hawaiian Islands. A fire destroyed the city of Lahaina so far killing 114, with over 800 victims still missing. However, the local people know it is much higher for people and children missing and unaccounted for.

This specific timeline report was just days old of this fire devastation in Maui, Lahaina. The people are still shocked and grieving, hoping to find their loved ones.

It is still not factually known how the fire started. However, so many suspicious incidents and questionable timing. Such as government federal meetings.

The FEMA Feds are staying in a high-end hotel during their investigation of the fire incident. Governor Green's executive rezoned the law he passed. FEMA and Redcross community with countless Lahaina locals state these entities prevented any donated food, supplies, and donations meant to help the survivors. Stating the Governor, the Feds, and Maui police countless questionable acts of pre-fire incidence, during, and post-fire incidences.

Strangely, the Maui Chief of Police John was also the acting coroner. Other civilians stated Maui police intentionally prevented vehicles from exiting out of the front street during the fire devastation which caused deaths. Another coincidence was the island siren did not sound. Elementary schools were closed, and children were home.

In the days following, Governor Green held community meetings that focused on house developers to discuss the rebuilding of Lahaina all without Lahaina community leaders and community residents, etc.

The many suspicious have not received satisfactory answers and yet the community leaders demand accountability for the lives lost and homes gone.

Yet the Government has been trying to move the Lahaina town building and open Maui to tourists, all with no responsibility or accountability for the catastrophic devastation.

Evidence and Conjecture

It is clearly noted that there are so many suspicious underlinings that trust is a huge issue. This clearly shows a different agenda for those who are supposed to be trusted. However, actions of greed and financing profiting were being played out in the first stage of rebuilding Lahaina without the community leaders who truly represented the Islands' best intention for the Lahaina community.

The point still is not to bash and point fingers at those known possibly as responsible.

Instead, it's about doing the right thing and resolving these issues in a civilized process. It is those who are wrong and have some kind of responsibility to own up to it and be accountable.

In January 2023, there was a community meeting regarding the future development of Smart Cities. A map of Maui shows Lahaina is on the map as a smart city location.

Hawaii's Governor Green the same week of the fire held a meeting with housing developers that were asked the approval to fast-track, to rebuild Lahaina without the Lahaina Kanaka-Maoli coalition and Lahaina community leaders involved.

Most importantly, the understanding with people of culture and Mana, there isn't enough money that can replace the reasons why we do what we do.

Why we live.
Why we work.
Why we love.
Why we do what we do.
Why we feel.
Why we feel what we feel.

These reasons must be relevant in our civil society and agreed conditions using the two pillars of civility.

1. To treat others the way you want to be treated.
2. If the shoe were on the other foot.

So, if our family, loved ones, and friends have suffered hurt, or killed, or negative things happened to your children, would you not hope the two pillars were applied?

Just like the Kanaka Maoli's indigenous natives to Hawaii, it is their belief and history that something different took place.

Queen Lili'uokalani was forced by the United States, a powerful military nation, to keep the Hawaiians in check and imprisoned at her palace.

They had to follow the same engagement that the United States President and Congress did to the Hawaiians that they did to the native Indians. How they were killed off, taken off prime lands, and displaced in desolate lands.

The Native Indians incident happened centuries ago, yet we are seeing it played out again in 2023 in Maui, Lahaina.

Philosopher George Santayana said, "Those who cannot remember the past are condemned to repeat it."

Government to the Cultural Ethnicities

Today in 2024, I do not care what side one stands on Political party wise. When the government supersedes culture by continuing to increase taxes or supersede laws on American minority territories and island states, anything and everything, especially from America, can and will become a trust factor by those people affected.

These people most of the time feel excluded and have no voice to hold on to what they worked so hard to have. The legislative laws already drain the pockets of the local people who are not subsidized in the cost-of-living factor, yet the increase of government inflation affects them through taxation of imports and export goods.

These parts of American states and territories are basically impossible to live within those means of low wages. What is notable in the modern government and political push point black is greed and power control.

Today, more than ever, there are career politicians who are 20-40 years still serving as senators, house representatives, or congress members, living comfortability high on the hog paychecks that they vote on to increase our taxes.

Sadly, the fox who has been placed to watch the hen house has been by-passing stupid laws that allow these corrupt politicians not only to advance themselves but also pass laws that hold them not liable as countless others' businesses who send other common citizens to jail for doing the same thing.

These passed laws allow them to act and enrich their greed and power. Meanwhile, for the common layman, our cultural outcome is affected by disappointing higher taxes and no accountability.

Because of these types of government and political greed taxes brought on by greedy agendas, negative, wasteful spending, and keeping the common citizen enslaved has been the common practice. These forced tax hikes to pay whatever these corrupted politicians pass through legislative legal laws mingled with their dark, greedy agendas are no longer being hidden.

Sadly, more than ever, it is necessary to live and perpetuate the cultural foundation of our positive cultural attributes of civility. If we can look back at the past generations when culture and gifts from the heart did not cost them anything because it was made from the sacrifice of hard work and from the heart.

Education

Sadly, an issue that is being played out by our Millennials, Gen-Z, and Alpha generation is that of schools, colleges, and universities that are indoctrinating our youth to hate their own country.

While other communist, dictators, and socialist nations such as China, Russia, Iran, North Korea, Palestinians, etc. teach their youth to love, support, and be patriots of their country.

Many of these Ivy League schools, colleges, universities, and educational systems are funded by billionaires such as George Soros, Klaus Schwabe, and Bill Gates just to name a few who see America in a very different light that plays second fiddle to their world plan of one world domination.

Plan Attacks on innocent lives

Most recently, in October 2023 a very controversial argument that got a nation more divided was the fact that the main news media reported

Hamas terrorist organization living in Palestine invaded parts of Israel, which was under the Palestine and Israel First and Second Intifada Oslo Accords.

It appears for thousands of years that Palestine and Israel have always feuded over the land, especially the recognized area of Jerusalem, which had great significant meaning to both nations.

Through centuries, various nations have attempted to broker a peace deal between the two nations who seemed to be on and off war for injustice in areas for their people which included both nations. Even specialized areas where neither nation agreed to control still resulted in issues, it always led back to war and bloodshed.

I believe and it is reasonably understood that during war, countless people are killed. No nation should intentionally commit genocide by murdering and butchering innocent people and/or babies, regardless of the age of the war.

I believe on the world stage the Geneva Convention has rules of engagement for war regardless of who is involved on a world stage to treat prisoners and or citizens with humanity.

The main news media reported and showed the inhumanity of the shocking massacre of Israeli soldiers being murdered, citizens being burned, and babies being shot and decapitated all within their known Israel homeland territory leaving a wake of 1000 Israelis dead during a concert or sitting in their homes.

The shocking follow-up here in the United States because of what the Hamas terrorist organization did was supported by a shocking percentage of far-left liberal professors and students from Ivy League colleges and universities all mostly from democratic states such as New York, Chicago, Masseuses, Washington DC, California which includes middle eastern and other sympathetic students who protested the United States for supporting Israel.

The alarming thought is the pointing out of the students blaming the massacre on the Israelites for occupying Palestinian land, so they had it coming to them. It's their fault.

What I find disturbing is the fact that it was not war, it was indeed murder and genocide as hatred for another race. You cannot say it's injustice if the shoe were on the other foot. Meaning that the Israelites did the same thing to Hamas citizens, families, and babies, which was inhuman.

No one can deny that the Israeli military's reactions to these atrocities are warranted and justifiable. If you do, then you're a hypocrite. Regardless, I will see nothing as good and or support the actions of killing innocent people or nations. Even if it's the American military power which I will be the first to share has its fair share of world responsibilities to be accountable for.

Charity Never Fails

If someone does not have any expectation of a gift given from the heart, they can never be offended. Humility is a key attribute of seeing great blessings. Humility invokes pure love and is what we need in our nation, our cultures, and our personal lives to be more unified.

Charity, humility, and love will offend no one. When someone in our American culture is giving from their heart regardless of how cheap or strange a gift, maybe it will not be offensive.

I urge people of cultural nations to return to those traditions that share charity, humility, and love. From the past lays the future.

In those days, they were self-reliant and gave what they could, even if it was made from the surroundings of their environment. The culture's creative thoughts **made do with what you had**. Today, it has changed with what you can buy that is expensive.

I can recall the words of my older brother who was thrifty to make things work. He said to me during Christmas that 'presents are something you buy when you cannot give of your true self.

Today, more than ever, I see this truth being underlined during holidays, especially with both parents or single parents who cannot be at home raising their children because taxes and inflation make it unaffordable to stay home and raise your children.

These politicians, when running for office, all guarantee for taxes that things will change once they get in. Then once these politicians get voted in, they jump on the bandwagon of increasing taxes and make excuses about their responsibilities.

These politicians seem to get comfortable in their positions, feeling they are held to a different standard and that they do not have any responsibilities and accountabilities.

In the business culture, the political people are not held to any standards except if they receive donations, they are expected to honor whatever agreement was made regarding the business donation.

As to ethnicity and culture, it is with slight minor changes for the cultured people. They expect that the politicians who pleaded for the community votes and support listened and promised to make changes that affect their communities and their cultures. Sadly, money speaks louder than culture and lives.

Especially recently notable during the changes of worldly influences and forced medical mandates from the coronavirus pandemic where government protocols pushed these mandates through the medical platform of the CDC and WHO insisting that it was from these medical platforms.

People's choices, whether on the island or off, were being forced to receive this untested human vaccine. Especially affected people from all cultures and walks of life if they wanted to fly from one country to the United States. Shots were mandatory.

Patriots serving in the military, federal, state, and county workers; and again, all cultures and walks of life, even if your religion did not believe such undertaking of the vaccines, people lost their livelihood to feed their families if they did not accept the mandate of vaccines.

When these medical mandates are issued by the government to influence their business employees to receive the vaccine shots, this leaves no choice.

My question is how this nation is governed by liberty, freedom, and justice for all when the government is mandating actions of no choice against its citizens.

The Polynesian people and culture whose structure has been created, reshaped and changed because of the past non-Polynesian arrivals, environments, or life-changing construct such as medical issues which created effects on the islands such as schooling and religion by the Colonial British, Germans, Chinese, and the American powers during times of war.

In the past centuries, the Chinese and Koreans have had a tremendous influence and effect on the Samoan people and generational construction of the environment. Technology, on a slow-moving island, also brings changes to island and when Polynesians left their motherland and were introduced to other cultures and their influences on island causing cultural gaps (changes) in the fabric of the Polynesian culture and belief lived.

I have always advocated for my parents as mentors. My biological father was never around for me. My mother remarried and my stepfather raised me as a respected high chief who branded the Samoan culture in our homes. I learned the pros and cons of our culture.

The generation of Polynesian people or Islander persons lives, understands, relates, and or identifies with the Polynesian culture. I shared in no disrespectful way that the villagers needed to have a voice so they could be heard. My stepfather would say that he was bound to the culture protocols as a high chief.

In short, regardless of where you were born, in the homeland of the Polynesian islands or elsewhere, overseas or states side. Regardless of whether speaking or understanding the Polynesian languages taught or not, or, if one adapted the culture within the walls of your home, it is all-important to us personally.

Chapter 3

RECOGNIZING GAPCULOGY AS AN INCLUSIVE CULTURAL LIFESTYLE

Gapculogy is inclusive as a recognized cultural lifestyle.

Being raised or even adopted into the Polynesian culture is a specific foundation like the spirit of God, that the culture is caught not taught.

I honestly believe that regardless of what specific Polynesian background one comes from this list of five attributes I share would be the same for all Polynesians: Love for God, love for family, respect for the elderly, love for culture, and standing proud of who you are and represent.

I believe if you ask any Polynesian or Islander 10 out of 10 times, they will name the same five attributes that describe their culture, I mentioned. However, a big negative characteristic is **hypocrisy.**

Hypocrites–'Do what I say, not what I do.'

If the culture is used to display Polynesian cultured tattoos or Polynesian products which are noted on any of the anatomy exterior (limb), rather than living as a product of the Polynesian culture in (life), then you know as to the beliefs of your identity and what is considered a necessity may be confused where to look on the outside or on the inside heart. The difference in belief is that we are trying to look like Polynesians or living the Polynesian culture.

I am not against anyone living their culture by showing their cultured tattoos to me. I wear it in my heart and my cultured beliefs.

The Samoan observed article shared Su'a Suluape Petelo, a renowned Samoan master tattooist has decried the continued abuse of the traditional art which he says is disrespecting Samoan culture.

Instances where a female is inked with a tatau, which is traditionally meant for men, and a fa'afafine (male who believes she's a female) getting the malu which is meant for women has not gone down well with Sua Suluape Petelo.

Su'a led his assistants and together with the Malofie group of men with traditional tattoos or 'tatau' inked people as part of their Malofie Exhibition at the Samoa Tourism Authority Fale on Friday, while focusing on teaching the students about the values and the history of the tatau.

In an interview with the media, Su'a said he firmly believes that as a traditional tattooist with many years of service to the country, doing a tatau on a woman will destroy and disrespect the bond between the tufuga (traditional tattooist) and a woman.

Doing a malu on a fa'afafine, according to the master tattooist, is also disrespectful to the culture and its history and to the Samoan ancestors who started the tatau.

"I will never accept a fa'afafine coming to me to get a malu and I have never in my years of doing this done that before," he said. "I had an older brother who tattooed a tatau on a woman and no one was happy about it.

"I was even more disappointed and asked him why he did what he did, but he said it was because no one had done it before.

Then the next thing we knew, he got into an accident and died, and I told his children that this was the real reason he died because karma never sleeps, and he did harm to the culture.

"Not only it's inappropriate to the culture but also to our traditions because if a girl wants to get a tatau, what would the tufuga feel towards her having to see all private parts of her body, which he shouldn't and that's why a tatau is for men and a malu is for women."

Su'a also appealed to all Samoans to put more pride into their culture by wearing their traditional tattoos for their love of the culture and "not for show".

He then not only stressed the essence and value that the tatau holds and carries but also the changes brought about by the ever-changing Samoa today and the technological revolution.

“The goal is for more people to wear this Samoan treasure with pride,” he said.

> ***Amidst our unity, hypocrisy remains a stark adversary. We must embrace our cultural heritage not merely through external symbols, but by embodying its values within our hearts and lives.***

When asked about the growing number of Samoans getting the traditional tattoo, Su’a said he is happy to see many young Samoans stepping forward with the courage to get inked.

“The good thing is seeing more of the females coming forward to get inked with the traditional tattoo and there’re more women than men,” he said.

Su’a leads the Malofie Association of Tattooists and men and women with traditional tattoos who were inked by Su’a and his assistants.

There are currently 15 traditional tattooists working alongside Su'a including his three sons and a woman.

I have worked professionally for decades, wearing a badge and carrying a firearm. I always use the analogy that just because you carry a firearm does not mean you have to use it in all situations.

In life, we will always have our views and truths. We will always face disagreements because everyone's perspective varies based on their personal experiences in life, which become their truth. I have learned through countless experiences in life to pick my battles. Going back to the foundation of happiness.

Chapter 4

CHOOSING HAPPINESS OVER BEING RIGHT

Do I want to be right, or do I want to be happy?

When our foundational beliefs seem as easy as choosing between black and white yet we're living in a world of gray.

We start to be more selective about only fighting for our foundational true core, which is righteousness. That makes one unique regarding truth and belief.

Truth is based on the doctrines of God, not man's policies. Doctrines of God do not change. However, policies do change to better fit the narrative and environment of changes in generations and cultures.

Abundance versus Scarcity

In past Generations as kids, we looked up to our grandparents and parents (Tupuna's and Kapuna's) grandparents or people from the older generation tried to make life easier for us.

As kids and youths, we looked to them for advice because they were more experienced in life, and seemed to always have things we wanted. They always knew things we had no clue about, what to do and when to do it. **They made things easier for us.**

Unfortunately, years later, the concern for us as a grown-up generation would result negatively.

Across the board of generations, we did not know it. Most of the time, we did not understand the value or great worth of things handed to us by our past generation.

As kids of innocent, naive, and inexperienced mentality, countless times, our grandparents or parents or guardians spoiled us because they loved us.

However, when a person from an older experienced generation gives something of value to another person who does not understand a value, that what they gave was acquired or earned through efforts of time, sacrifice, and work, it will not be appreciated or valued the same way.

As an example, let's take candy. As a kid, I loved candy. I still love and enjoy my chocolate Snickers candy bar.

As a kid, I had no money, and my parents were not rich. Every time I heard my mom was going to the store, I would run out and jump in the car with the intention of getting me some candy.

My mom would always tell me, "Son, I don't have any extra money." I did not care nor did I pay attention to my mom's words. I heard her but still got my way.

I got in the car and no; I did not understand the value of the money. I just knew and expected from my experience that I could talk Mom into getting candy, especially if I whine or cry.

As an adult, I heard a talk given by Neal A Maxwell, an apostle for the Church of Jesus Christ of Latter-Day Saints. Maxwell stated, **"People who choose easy things and easy ways in life make them weak."**

Regardless of whether or not a person is of faith, this statement is filled with worldly experiences that ring true to the core.

The issue of the generations before is that they're always trying to create an easier way for the next generation that follows.

My grandparent's generation lived in huts with other family members. They were raised on the Samoan islands and did not have the luxury to work, or go to school and be educated because of a world war.

Depression, hunger, and struggles were the norms. Yet they kept the hope and made the best of a negative, harsh life.

My parent's generation was also raised in the Samoan islands and lived in their own hut. Limited in education. They worked hard for a little money in jobs they hated. They climbed trees and fished for food.

They dug deep pits in the ground to cook meat and used bathrooms outside. Their parents' generation made it easier for them to live.

My generation was born in Hawaii, and raised in a house with a bathroom and running water. I was educated in schools and college in California. I ate fast food. I could work what I wanted to do as a profession and enjoy life.

As a baby boomer parent now, who was taught by my parents' silent generation, I want my children's millennial and Z-generation to have better ideas for their timeline and future generations.

I want to make it easier for my children to live by teaching them what I share is my truth, not theirs. Now my question is "Knowing this is not their truth but my truth that I share, will it be any easier for our children to understand?"

My children's generation will not have things easier than when we did because they are still learning what their truths are.

Many Kids and youths raised by family and culture grow up feeling like they are the enemy.

'The enemy that **looks** like me.'
'The enemy that **speaks** like me.'
'The enemy that **thinks** like me.'

If Culture is not taught correctly, it can cause our future posterity to lose their identity feeling shame, they do not fill the demanding cultural expectations.

In the course of my growing up in America, such was my case. Being a Samoan who does not speak the Faa Samoan language. By the homeland-raised Samoans, I was viewed as an aspiring to be a Palagi (white man).

Creating a culture takes time.

Creating a culture takes a safe space.

Creating a cultural language takes patience and understanding.

When creating a culture, a platform of learned growth and progression for the best, the resources and people must be the best and at their best.

Evidence and Perspective

However, the big disconnect for us is we did not have cell phone computer technology in our time growing up.

Since 1988, everything I knew as a baby boomer and my spouse's Generation-X changed overnight. Suddenly, the millennial generation became the first generation to live and adapt to the touch and click of a mouse on the internet. Schools, food, employment, social media, etc. came online connections.

The baby boomers and Gen-X started raising their kids, the millennials, in a non-confrontational way, along with using the television to babysit children.

We started teaching our children that they can become anything they want. When they would become disobedient instead of punishments or spankings, we put them on timeout.

As these millennials grew into young adults, they started coming across as entitled to what they wanted and did not want to work for it. These millennials do not appreciate what they have been given.

Perspectives

My Grandfather walked to work 10 miles.

My Father walked 5 miles.

I drove a Cadillac.

My Son or Daughter will drive a Mercedes.

My Grandson or Granddaughter will drive a Ferrari.

My Great grandson or granddaughter will be walking.

Huh' walking! why is that?

He said to me ...

Tough Times Create Strong People.

Strong People Create Easy Times.

Easy times Create Weak People.

Weak People Create Tough Times.

He said we need to raise warriors.

Shocked to hear a friend ask this specific question, "Why do we care about what happens to our posterity after we die?" Imagine all those children, including your tree line, a fighting chance of being warned by someone who has been through the gauntlet of life.

Sadly, millennials and Z-Generation have become lazy and not a matter of if, but when life's result will not be kind or unforgiving and cause such a harsh lesson. What will they do when tough times hit them? I pray and hope they understand the metaphor of the message just shared about tough times.

I see the attitude of these younger generations and if they do not change; I see they will either fail because when turmoil hits, they will flounder in life and sink or they will learn the hard way what is needed is the action of prevention.

However, our experiences from the past must be satisfied with knowing that failing is part of progress. God has brought us through our challenges, trials, and tribulations which are meant for us to learn to understand little by little that there come times in our lives when we get thrown into the pool and need to either swim or sink.

That said, I shared the truth that only those who have experienced tough times are strong people. Easy times create weak people. They can relate to these truths.

Traditional Tainted by Intraculture

Example: One of the oldest forms of leadership is alive and **The Chieftain (Matai) System** in the homeland and beyond the Polynesian culture lifestyle of protocol has even changed.

However, as much as these powerful countries attempted to change all Polynesian cultures, gratefully today, my Polynesian culture has not been wiped out and is still actively alive and implemented.

Still, the chieftain system of high chiefs and talking chiefs who still act as overseer orators on behalf of the recognized culture.

The Samoan culture recognizes the 'Matai system' aka Chieftain system (filled with high chiefs and talking chiefs). The Matai system oversees the culture in all matters of importance regarding disputes, or recognition of title, especially such as a Samoan wedding or funeral.

The family protocol at such events allows the family chief to be recognized and they recognize other chiefs during the events.

The protocol is that the chiefs stand as orators and speak the history and recognitions for and on behalf of the family. To me, these moments seem more about chiefs showing off with who's better with elegant words of persuasion.

Meanwhile, the rest of the family members have no voice in this protocol.

This point can be argued, but who will listen? The culture has a system that only the Chiefs or parents to their children again that is on the islands.

In other countries, for the families who move there, the culture is still the foundation within the home and heart. The teachings are still recognized wherever you go by the Polynesians. However, it is not and causes more harm than good.

In 2022, at Salt Lake City, Utah, there was a Polynesian leadership meeting of Samoan, Tongan, Hawaiian, Cook Island, Māori, and Tahitian roundtable after three Samoan teenagers in their communities were gunned down by other minorities.

The meeting brought American Samoan Congress Woman, Amua Amata Radenwagen, Utah Attorney General, Sean Reyes Hawaiian-Filipino, and me to talk and share solutions with leadership.

The parents who attended had valid worries about the future of their children's safety.

When a question was asked to AG Reyes what parents can do to help their children stay out of trouble. AG Reyes called on my expert perspectives as a Dr. in Philosophy, Polynesian, father, and expert with youth intervention.

I simply shared the relatable factors that most of us in this room are first-generation citizens of this great nation and now parents and grandparents.

Culture in this New Age Needs to Change

Change today does not mean we dishonor and disrespect our Matai's, Ali'is, Kapuna's. As we reflect on our chief's and their leadership voice, we listen to daily, which is that of our parents and grandparents who absolutely know what we need. They brought us here to the place where we currently live, whether we are born on an island or off island.

In their time, their education was limited compared to what off island power could offer. That said, we honor our parents and grandparents as they were intuitive (wise) enough to know that the motherland's future was limited, and they wanted to provide hope and more opportunities for their posterity.

I am grateful as my mother shared that she loved her children and their father at the time the family was brought to the United States. Her experience was that she listened to and learn from other family members living in America. A nation filled with hope and opportunities.

My Parents knew it would not be easy living in another country, but whatever sacrifices needed to be made, they felt it would be worth it.

For me, the takeaway of changes can be easily seen in how the next generation prepares a funeral service for their past generation of parents and elders.

The Five Building Blocks of Civility for the Next Generation

What is the Cultural Future Objective?

Any change in our personal lives as to our habits and expectations is never easy. What is even more, pinnacle doubts are changes when it comes to culture. For Polynesian the word Taboo or sacred is aligned and enthralled as a lifestyle!

If culture is changed within the household without the support of the parents or guardian, it may be easier to slide maybe a small act here and there.

However, if culture is changed without the overseeing approval of family or village high chiefs, it is more than likely you will not get away from what it will amount to as disrespecting the culture.

Culture is systematically in charge. It is the foundation of posterity and life. It is required for the survival of all cultures. Change of tradition seemingly is never warranted, but if it will assure the survival of culture for the betterment of its people, then in my judgment it is needed.

If I moved off the island with my family to another land to reside for whatever reason, the very surroundings of the neighbors we moved are cemented by people who despise and hate people of different cultures and looks.

Did I mention that the police are afraid to patrol in that neighborhood because of the violence and the lack of support they get? Your kids are harassed in the neighborhood and in school daily because of their love for culture.

Sadly, I would be a bad example because I do not care how outnumbered I would be. I would be at war every day kicking teeth in. However, when my kids are involved, my thoughts change. Moving to another location or back to an island would be my decision.

To say to your kids to stop living your culture is like telling them to stop breathing. The Hawaiian culture translates their culture as such. 'If there is no life, there are no presences.'

For example, the Hawaiian word 'Aloha', when shared, can suggest three outcomes: hello, goodbye, or I love you, depending on how you say it, or whom you say it to.

Now take the word 'Aloha' when broken down into two syllables, it has an innate infinitive understanding and meaning. The first syllable 'Alo' is defined as (the presence of).

And 'Ha' is defined as (the breath of life). This is where the understanding 'if there is no life, there is no presence' comes from.

Most Polynesians, if not all, share the same cultural perspective of facts and understanding. That all things first flow with a spiritual understanding before any thoughts of cultural change.

In the Old Testament, we read in the book of Genesis 19: 24-26, how Lot and his family were warned by two angels to leave a city in which they grew up, that God was going to destroy Sodom and Gomorrah because of its iniquity.

The time was at hand and the angels told them to depart out of the city and not look back. While the lord destroyed Sodom and Gomorrah, lot's wife turned and looked back and as she did so, she turned into a pillar of salt and calcium.

Why do I share this? Let us consider Lot's wife's action. After the angels warned Lot and the family to not look back. And yet Lot's wife did so.

The thought that comes to mind is that this city of life is all Lot's wife and family knew. They were told not to look back, but she did. Culture is important and as important as the breath of life.

However, when pinnacle moments in life change, so must we. How many of us did not want to change a thing during the COVID-19 pandemic but did because of what the results may be?

Today, we are the recipients of a future of hope and change. I thank my parents for the sacrifices they made. I gladly state with gratitude not just my parents but all parents who sacrificed for their family and children, and I boldly state that it was worth it! It changed our lives for the better.

Now, it's our time as parents to fight and sacrifice for our children's future, which is rapidly changing. And it is not a question of whether we need to sacrifice.

We must make sacrifices to ensure that our children have the required tools to progress and stand on their own feet for their future. We must, as parents, be educated and be relevant to today's challenges.

The answers to our parents' experiential truths of long ago do not and will not solve the worldly modern-day issues of today.

Today, we cannot answer anything we have never encountered.

Things like generational issues that have never been experienced such as the CV19 or the pandemic. The pandemic resulted in an onslaught of youth's mental health or communication negatively affected.

In most cases of such responses by parents who were once told by their parents to just be tough and that they would get through it, parents answered because they did not really have the answer.

Today, after past teachings from our parents, the answer is simply listening to learn, then learning to listen to the communication health process.

This means listening to our children's issues. Do not think you know better about their issues that you have never experienced or know anything about.

Instead, support them by finding ways to better understand our children's experiential truths and their issues.

Sunday, day of rest

Another example in Samoa of influence by colonization is the Christian missionaries. Imagine that in 2023, we are still living the remnant of influential beliefs that on the Samoan islands, and on Sundays around 6 pm in all the villages, it shuts down out of respect for curfew time for family prayers.

In Samoa, this happens. The villagers take the culture seriously, so when you are not supposed to be on the village road driving, the villagers will intervene, and it may not be a good thing if you ignore the curfew time.

Now imagine trying to live your Polynesian cultural roots off-island and trying to enforce family prayer time in your local American community. It would not happen because most non-Polynesian people would not recognize this or honor it.

Each Polynesian Island and culture has its own identity and unique cultural roots.

So, imagine Polynesian or Pacific Islanders like me who are raised off-island, to recognize wherever we're living.

Imagine being raised off the island as a citizen of that country in a crowded metropolis, with influence by multiple cultures, and being taught by the government, schools, or people of different influences that your cultural history is in that place you only know as home.

Living as Afa kasi a Polynesian/Asian mixed American lifestyle can be confusing.

Priorities of Educational Influences

When we harbor multiple areas of influence, when or where do our priorities need to come into play? Well, it is always easier to say, "Don't worry, I got this."

Let's say that most times with the reality experienced off the island or wherever, we will deal with multiple areas of multitasking of learning and studying things of our culture and education.

If we are multitasking, how does that help to increase our focus? In my experiential truth, you would be lucky to engage even 30% percent of culture and education, which if it is a higher percentage, would be related to a sport of 55% that you play which focuses on interweaving education and culture.

Such as the reason for Polynesians who are highly sought and vetted for their commitments in sports from high schools, and colleges to the NFL because of their size, speed, strength, talents, and love of family respect.

Football is a huge draw for Polynesian kids, which allows the individual to use their culture and talents to be showcased, especially in high-contact sports arenas.

Polynesian educational studies seem to drop a great percentage when compared to the mainstream of the culture upbringing.

The fact that sports seem to be not just a way but how Polynesian athletes are being aggressively pursued contractually to play for professional teams, so Polynesian or Pacific islanders use their talents to focus on becoming professional athletes and making a living.

The data shows Polynesian athletes' educational proficiency indicates that 4 out of 20 Polynesians meet the requirements and end up doing well in the profession. While the rest who do not make studying a priority fall short or the wayside.

If Polynesian athletes focused on education studies that increased their mental strategy, simply by being more patient and prepared, studies show that a person, such as a valedictorian, uses their time more abundantly to focus on studying.

However, the truth remains to accomplish such a task; the standard is already set high; and unless you are already used to such high tasks and can deal with the stress that comes along, you must also deal with time, studies, and focus. Now throw in after-school sports where that commitment of time is a necessity.

This is where many Polynesian sports athletes fall by the wayside, including yours truly. I recall as a college football player who played on the 1983-84 National Championships team and Pony Bowl championship team back-to-back. It was my dream to make it to the NFL.

But to my dismay, what did I expect if I did not take studying seriously? Like a knucklehead, I thought I was good enough just to have a pure talent that I did not need to study.

Yes, my limited thoughts ended my football career because I thought wrong. I found my choices limited, grateful for my talents. I made a career in Polynesian dancing working for Disney company for a decade before becoming a professional SAG actor/stuntman in film and television production.

If I could do it all over again, I would change the knucklehead attitude I had and focus on education studies.

Hopefully, I am impressed with the need to prepare for your future. Dear Athletes, take education and studies seriously. I cannot echo the importance of focusing on studying and realize that your focus studies will be put to the test, studies cut down to a bare minimum.

We assume that focused study time has been cut down, but let us now add getting a part-time job.

This cuts into one's study time with less opportunity to focus on studying to become not a valedictorian but just a B-average student. A 4.0 GPA gets your talents in any college door for a full-ride scholarship.

The point is not just Polynesians, but we, as human beings, cannot keep focused on just one thing while trying to do multiple things—an act known as multitasking. The reasons come down to not being able to control our thoughts as it certainly and easily wanders off course.

In my limited understanding, and my faith in God. This topic falls under trusting the Savior Jesus Christ's teachings, who warns us in Matthew 6:24, "No Man can serve two masters: for either he will hate the one and love the other, or else he will hold to the one and despise the other. Ye cannot serve both God and mammon."

Serving two masters at the same time can place us with the same mindset of not focusing, allowing our minds to wander on many issues that do not help us and instead interrupt our direct and clear focus.

When our mind wanders, only 30 percent of our focus is on play, and it causes problems for us all. And with that, our happiness is at stake. Consider a racing car engine being given 100 percent horsepower to use.

However, only 30 percent of its horsepower is what we must function on in the race. Consider those around us in the race who are using even 65 percent to 80 percent and consider those using 80 percent of their think tank to our wandering 30 percent.

This does not even put us in the race. Compare how you use your think tank at the workplace and school by listening, learning, and resolving concerns and issues. Using only 30 percent, we can consider it's not our best day.

Not allowing our think tank to be 100 percent functional, I am sure you can consider the results.

Dreams

I see Polynesians straight from the islands seem to take studies more seriously. I believe it is because they feel they have much more to lose than those Polynesians and Islanders who live in the States.

I love this point. Stay determined and never give up on your dreams.

Influencing Our Cultures and Future Generations

As a strong-willed person during the coronavirus pandemic, there were drastic orders or mandates of change that I compared to President Lincoln's quote, giving lives to save a limb. The pandemic in my experiential culture life changed how we lived.

I consider the fact that decades before this pandemic, we have had previous outbreaks of viruses such as Mad Cow Disease, Zika, and Sars just to name a few.

I do not recall in the United States during these outbreaks a mandate to stop all businesses, schools, and all non-essential functioning lives and lifestyles needing to shut down.

Americans and all citizens in the US were forced to stop living life as we all knew it and go home and isolate. Shutting down businesses and ways of life caused the loss of lives only to save a limb. The decision made by our government and mandated was to save the limb, this made no sense.

All the American citizens were told to get the jab (vaccine). First, they did not take into consideration our rights regarding medical history. Religious beliefs. There was also that little thing called our constitutional rights.

The Jab information put out by the government was that if you got the vaccine, you would be protected from the deadly coronavirus. Sadly, it turned out not to be true, and the narrative changed.

Through my research, I learned that the vaccine did not go through the correct protocol of testing like all vaccines' normal protocol. The vaccine was never tested on people. The data results showed that it was only tested on selected animals.

Indeed, it was rushed out, and in the process, many people who received the vaccine died. And many who received the vaccine, including many in my family, also caught the coronavirus still and they got sick.

I had caught the CV-19 four times in three years, and only once did it put me down on my deathbed for a month. After taking Ivermectin and hydroxychloroquine while on my deathbed, I testify these pills are the antidote.

Ivermectin and hydroxychloroquine had and not to mention I researched them and not surprisingly, they worked for the previous century. According to the CDC, ivermectin scientists in 2018 were awarded the Nobel Peace Prize.

Shockingly, during this pandemic outbreak, these medications were now banned, and it made no sense. It saved my life. After taking it for five days straight, I was back on my feet. Within two weeks of recovering and back to work at my full-time job.

During the pandemic, when all the children in school were sent home to quarantine and isolate, I disagreed and felt it would harm many children who were at the mercy of being isolated and having unlimited access to negative social media platforms.

Many parents were not equipped to help their children with tools through these crises. Many domestic disputes were occurring and our children found the social media platforms a daily go-to which became a mental health-related contributor, being the kids had no social media boundaries.

The internet was the only thing they could engage in daily, no longer able to play with friends or family members.

The internet has become the playground for our children. It became their community. **The problem** that was never considered by adults was that these innocent, naïve, and inexperienced minds who were already plagued with fear and limited boundaries continued to spiral towards anxiety, stress, and depression disorder.

The social media platform was a breeding ground for negative effects. These innocent, naïve, and inexperienced minds of our children during the pandemic were like shooting fish in a barrel.

Kids, while on the social media platforms, did not know any better, and countless found themselves cyberbullied. During the pandemic, cyberbullying ramped upward including an uptick in suicides. This result was another perspective of taking lives to save limbs.

Due to the mental health disorders that resulted, especially for the Millennials and Z-Generation.

For centuries years, so many questions, debates, divisions, agendas, anger, chaos, protest, destruction, pandemics, forced mandates, death, blame, challenges, trials, and tribulations have plagued our earth.

Many past Generations such as the Greatest Generation, the Silent Generation, the GI Generation, and the Baby Boomers, have lived long enough to identify, experience, and adjust to the negative challenges, trials, and tribulations.

Due to this reason, I am so grateful and blessed to have learned the foundation of civility. "If You receive Hostility, Use Civility."

The definition of civility is summed up simply as being civil one to another, regardless of being amid challenges, trials, or tribulation. Allowing humanitarian reasons to flourish.

In this book, my focus is to share my experiential truths with all generations, especially the latest; millennials, Z-generation, and Alpha generational that when you are amid negative challenges, trials, and tribulations do not look to the older generations for answers because we have gone through countless experiences.

However, nothing is close to what this generation is experiencing. Their challenges are totally different.

By understanding, even for the young, innocent, naive, and inexperienced generations, these types of outcomes are part of the human experience, which has always found solutions.

When the world and national health leaders are rushing vaccines that have not been properly tested like it was, there are always consequences.

That said, on the news and social media, the WHO and CDC medical recognized health experts seem to take a different path of testing. The United States government also seems to take a different path to people's rights. They mandated people to get the vaccine-19 shots or lose their jobs.

The government started with medical employees in the hospitals. Federal, state, and city law enforcement and the military were all mandated to receive the vaccine shots or lose their jobs. To me, that is a huge red flag concern. It is against your constitutionally protected rights as a human being.

Now, for many citizens who died during the pandemic regardless of how they truly died, suspiciously seem to be listed when taken to the hospitals that they died of coronavirus.

Those who survived are now fired and out of work. Children and teens were out of school, ordered by the government to stay home and social distance. **These mandates, in my professional opinion, caused countless deaths.**

Samoan High Chief

A huge influence on my upbringing was that I grew up without my biological father. From the impressionable age of 5 years old to roughly 12 years old, I was without a father. When my mother remarried, my stepfather Fiamatai Tauati-Mataia, I was pretty upset because I did not want any man to marry my mother. I wanted my father. I remember there were many days I cried for my father, but to no avail. He never returned.

When Tauati-Mataia married my mother and moved into our house, a lot of things changed. I learned through my mother that my stepfather carried a Samoan cultured high chief title. He was all about living the culture that I or my siblings knew nothing about. All I knew was I had resentment about my mom being married to this man. I had resentment regarding the Samoan culture that all five of us kids were subjected to live within our home.

The contrast of living culture is two. I always felt that we should not be forced to live truths we do not believe. This brings resentment.

However, I also experienced that, though one may disagree with truths that you do not believe. Yet, the truth of the law of gravity will still be in effect as one step off a cliff.

As kids, my stepfather used to punish us the way he was raised. Hence, we used to get physical beatings. Our punishments were with anything our parents could get their hands on: belts, extension cords, whips, intense pinching of the inner thighs, thick heavy leather support belts, broomsticks, and high heels. I think you get the point.

My Mother totally supported my stepfather's vision of his title as a high chief. Although we lived in the United States, our Samoan culture was enthralled by all we did and the places we attended.

My dad would constantly wear his ea'faikonga (skirt rapping) along with other Samoans present whom dad was constantly meeting. Soon, the years passed and my stepfather became my mentor and the father who raised us kids.

Soon, Mom and Dad had another son, Alex. Over the years, my brother Allen and I seemed to be very engaged in learning about the cultures through the Polynesian entertainment shows. We were performers for decades at renowned theme parks and traveling all over the world.

We learned to speak and understand the various Polynesian languages and cultures that we came to represent during the countless entertainment shows and performances. We represented the Islands of Hawaii, Samoa, Tonga, Māori, Fijian, Rarotonga, and Tahiti.

The unique credibility of all our shows ended with the most exciting and dangerous dance, the Samoa fire-knife dance. This performance is based on warriors who, after slaying their enemies and decapitating their heads, carry them back into the village to show their supreme warrior masculinity.

Today, the fire-knife dance represents the boy who becomes a man and warrior for the village. These performances you must be focused and prepared to bring the heat, literally.

It was indeed an education and a wonderful blessing to travel around the world sharing, learning, and experiencing life through the countless performances of the various Polynesian cultures.

However, it was an even bigger blessing to learn about the various cultures from the countries we visited and how much similarity we all have as people of the universal connection of culture, language, and history is pride.

Listen to learn, then learn to listen

This simple but profound thought is easier said than done. It takes experiences in challenges, trials, and tribulations to relate, understand, adjust, and adapt. You cannot explain to someone something you have never felt or experienced.

You may ask, "Dr. Sid, are you suggesting that older people possess a greater knowledge?" I am saying that being older and more experienced; the answer is still, no!

Example: When my daughter turned 21 years old in June 2023, she told me that when she turned 13 years old, she was under extreme stress in middle school. Sadly, I can recall what I said to my daughter. "That if she wanted to feel real stress, she can pay the bills." As a father, I failed my daughter with my comments that waved her reality off.

When my daughter turned 18 years old, she and I got into a spat which led to her experiencing a panic attack. I freaked out, as she was having a hard time breathing and did not know how to communicate her feelings.

After things calmed down, I learned from my daughter that I had triggered a bad memory she experienced at the age of 13 years when I dismissed her.

She told me she knew from that time on she could never count on me, her father, to be there for her emotional support. To hear that, I was devastated.

> ***"Through a panic attack, I learned empathy and the importance of understanding others' struggles and cultural identity.***

I swiftly changed and made my children's issues my priority. I discovered through the pandemic that all three of my children were going through anxiety, stress, and depression disorders.

I learned through professional research that these disorders are real and will not pass without helping or arming those affected with mental health tools.

There was a time when we learned to be tough, and we will get through it. However, today's issues differ from those times. Today, parents need to be relevant in the ongoing learning changes through experiential truths.

If cannot relate to their issues, how can we help them with what they are experiencing? Or help with the communication health tools they need. Finally, I had to agree with my daughter that I did not know what I did not know, nor could I relate.

Gratefully today, our children are doing fine. They have communication health tools for their disorders if needed. If parents only tell their children what to do not knowing their issues, then they fail at **listening to learn, then learn to listen.**

I was driving by in my security cart when I saw a mother walking with her two children on the public sidewalk crying. In passing, I overheard her say, "I am sorry, Meja, that the restaurant threw away your doll you love." I spun around and swiftly pulled up to the mother. First, understand that this was a big conventional show occurring, and it was a miserable 110 degrees hot outside.

I asked the mother if she was okay. She replied with a heavy Spanish accent, "No! Today changed my daughter's life for the bad. I cried for my daughter because her comfort doll was left behind at a restaurant and I called last night, and they said they had her doll. I asked if they would hold the doll for us. We would come today and get it. We walked from our hotel almost a mile, only to be told when we got there that the doll was thrown away. I had to bring them in these conditions as we were here for my son's game. My husband cannot take off work, it costs a lot of money to get us here. And now my daughter will not speak, instead she will cry inside her mind that was her comfort doll."

Now, for those who just read what I experienced, let me ask you a question. "What did you just hear me say about the mother that was urgent as shared by her?"

The mother shared a lot of things, but if a mother is crying about what effects the doll has on her daughter, then it must be important. So, I asked the mother because it is what she did not say that I heard.

I asked her if her daughter had anxiety and depression. The mom looked at me and sobbed. She says, "How did you know?"

I told her to allow me drive them on my security cart to their hotel location because it was scorching hot. In my driving, I quickly shared how my children also have anxiety, stress, and depression disorders. It's hard to tell someone this about their child, afraid that they will look at your child differently. I gave the lady my number and told her if there was anything I could do to help with her kids, that she should call me and I would be happy to introduce her to my wife and kids.

Long story short, I found online a person selling dolls, and after work, I drove to pick one up. Drove home, picked up my family, and called the lady to meet us outside her hotel. I gave her daughter the doll and her eyes lit up and she began talking nonstop. "I love this beautiful doll. I will give her a name and dress her and take care of her like my mother took care of us when we were kids."

Parents and Guardians Are Key to Raising Children

Quote: "No success outside the home can compensate for the failure within the home."

Parent's communication with their kids within the walls of their homes is the key to providing solutions. Communication health is the learning-to-listen process. We cannot be shocked if we do not have a standard of listening at home. Our children will find others who will listen, with less good intentions, and if such is the case, then parents cannot blame anyone else.

Learning this should not just be a time-consuming task, but a natural way of allocating time to instill positive attributes in your children. Listen to learn, then learn to listen.

After the birth of a new baby that you hear for the first time cry. How do you know what the baby is crying for?

The normal reaction is that it does not matter. Why? Because your love reacts to picking up the baby and rock it back and forth slowly to soothe the baby from crying. Is it possible that your thoughts are maybe the baby just wanted to be held?

This is the process of learned experiences. The reality is this perspective does not look good for people who are unsympathetic and who are crying and just use harsh tones of dialogue to work out their own issues.

When we are raising our child or children or loved ones when a crisis occurs, our intervention is normal for a parent to want to help.

Regardless of where you go or what you're doing, this specific nurturing attribute taught in one's surrounding family care is used everywhere, even at work when someone needs a parent figure or mentor.

Mental Health Issues Case and Point

On February 22, 2022, at approximately 0530 hours, while driving in the mobile vehicle to open a gate on Las Vegas Boulevard. Upon arrival and standing directly in the center lane of the street was a male who I quickly avoided hitting. The term we use for people who are mentally challenged is 421A. This 421A was a black male in his 50s.

I immediately turned on the vehicle's red and blue flashers, so that other vehicles driving behind me could avoid running into me. The subject who was later identified as Michael stated, 'The Federal government told me to stay right here in the streets that I could not move, and if he should move, he would be killed.'

Without hesitation, I adopted a communicational approach, prioritizing active listening to gain knowledge and then applying that knowledge to improve my listening skills. Instead of jumping to conclusions, I wanted to confirm whether Michael had any mental impairments. I began asking questions that involved how a reasonable person would reply logically.

After asking Michael several questions, I confirmed that I was dealing with a mental health-challenged person regardless that it was someone's son.

Just a year prior, I had been certified in CIT crisis intervention training.

The short of this situation, I knew Michael would fall into the space of being helped by the state of Nevada. I requested the Las Vegas Metropolitan Police and paramedics to respond, as Michael still refused to leave the spot in the middle of the street. I know it would be just a matter of time before something bad happens.

Thirty minutes later, emergency medic response and Clark County Fire Department arrived and transported Michael to Spring Valley Hospital, and then legal 2k would document him for state care.

Why Life of Civility?

If there is life, there must be civility. If there is no civility, there is no order. And if there is no order, there is no law. If there is no law, there is no justice. If there is no justice, there is no happiness. If there is no happiness, there is no need for life.

Mental Health disorders are real. If officers or first responders are not educated to understand that each person, regardless of the mental health crisis, is still human currency to their loved ones, I feel it is important to take the time to ask questions to let these people with disorders have a voice and a worth living regardless of what they may be experiencing.

On another day and time, at work, I came across a female in her thirties wearing a tie-dye t-shirt and shorts standing in the middle of the sidewalk, seemingly eyes closed, asleep. I stopped and for a minute stood next to her to make sure she was ok.

I politely asked her if she needed medical care. She slowly opened her eyes, lifted her head towards me, and said, "No, I am ok. I am wiped out, tired from walking the streets all night." I asked her if she needed me to call someone, and she said, "Yes, please."

Then she went into her story that her father warned her that if she left Wisconsin to go to Las Vegas for addiction treatment, he knew it would not last and that he did not approve. Her father told her that if she went and left the medical addiction center to not call him if she got herself in trouble.

She ended by saying, "No, do not call my father. I am not finished exploring this drug addiction." Then she thanked me for just being kind and listening to her without judgment.

Fill in the Gaps

She shared how her much older parents, who are far along the path of life, do not understand her issues. As a parent, I can relate and have always believed that our vast experiences with our children place us as one who knows and can educate our younger posterity. And just like the generation before us who used their experiences as a result to share their truths and blanket our unknown questions or answers to our questions.

However, today's generation does not work because the challenges of my generation were far different and simpler than today's challenges. Today's challenges are more complex, and issues are rapidly changing all the time.

What works through all generations is civility and communication health skills, such as listening to learn and learning to listen.

It is important to relate that if my kids did not see the things I saw, or experienced, the things I did which have become my truth, then how is telling my kids who cannot relate going to become their truth without them experiencing any of it?

Instead, I had to adjust and say, "Well, in the norms, it should be understood." Then it hit me as a friend and I were chatting, and he said to me after I used that expression, "It's only normal." He shared something interesting that has supported my views when he said 'What is really normal.' For me, living becomes defined by my daily experiences and how they shape my understanding of what is typical.

My experiences are my truth. Your experiences are your truth. This teaching is the basis of truth. If we are civil, seeing other truths may not be the same as ours. Then Civility will work and thrive as a foundation that treats all fairly. I realize that my everyday experiences are not even close to everyone's normal day.

Example: Is a religious priest or nun, who's committed to serving God living in the monastery considered normal? The answer is no if it is being compared to the average citizen. However, it is considered normal if we are talking about religious faith goers preparing to enter the monastery.

My daughter shared in 2016 that she had anxiety, stress, and depression disorder and that she normally on a daily struggled with panic attacks. As I tried to assist my daughter while she was going through a bout of panic attacks, she asked me the million-dollar relatable question.

"Dad, do you know what a panic attack feels like?" I shared with her that I did. The truth is that I experienced a panic attack. So, yes, I know what they feel like and know that this is a real disorder.

What is Our Related Disorder?

2012, I experienced a panic attack that changed my life. I was at home watching my two young daughters who were 6 years and 10 years.

My wife had left for work. I was on the phone, focused on a business call. I recall being on the phone for some thirty minutes while my daughters were upstairs playing in their room.

I wanted to make sure all was fine. As I walked towards the front door, and noticed the screen door slightly ajar. It caught my attention.

The person I was talking to was placed on hold by me. I listened for a second to hear the girls playing upstairs and yet heard nothing. I thought maybe my daughters got bored and fell asleep.

I walked upstairs, and they were not in their room. I called out to them, but no response. I said if they were playing hide and seek to stop playing and come out. Again, no response.

Suddenly I panicked. I ran downstairs and bolted out the front door. I remembered that was ajar. As fast as I could haul outside and glanced down the street both ways, looking to see if my girls wondered outside or worst-case scenario taken.

I looked for any type of nearby car driving or movement of any sort. However, to my despair, I saw nothing.

I screamed out for my girls when suddenly I dropped my phone as my legs and knees locked up. Not in control, I fell to the ground and became tunnel-visioned. As I struggled to catch my breath, gasping for air became increasingly difficult. I tried to yell out for help, but I could not. I was struck was fear.

Overcome with emotion, I found myself crying and plagued by negative thoughts about my daughters. I lay on the ground frozen.

Finally, I thought to myself; I needed to relax, just breathe. I lay on the floor of my driveway, gathering my thoughts. It is necessary for me to regain my emotional balance. Once a few minutes had passed, I found myself able to move my legs. I sat up and took a deep breath.

Then suddenly, with a better mindset, the thought entered my mind. Earlier that morning, before my wife left for work, she said that my sister-in-law was going to stop by and pick up the girls.

I said it was not like her to just grab the girls and say nothing. I prayed and hoped that this was the case. I called my sister-in-law and was grateful the girls were with their aunty. I found out that my niece, who is the same age as my daughter, came and took them. They noticed me talking on the phone and walked away.

Takeaway: Yes, I experienced a panic attack and know what it feels like, and they are real.

If I never experienced this before, I would probably be one of those uneducated people who would say to someone with an anxiety, stress, or depression disorder, "Just be tough, you'll get over it."

As a father well along the path of life, I humbly learned that I needed to widen my mindset and understand that you cannot teach something if you never had that experience to know what others may go through. It is vital to your mindset to not dismiss others' claims without verifying either by you or by a professional. **By the way, I am talking about experience across the spectrum board.**

Afa Kasi (translated, half Polynesian half mixed)

I was born in Hawaii and raised in the mainland (Orange County, California.) I share my truth raised by my Samoan parents fluent speaking, limited educated, and raised seven children to five key attributes I treasure even still today. God, Love, Respect, Proud Culture, and Representation.

My experience in the motherland of Samoa. It's worth mentioning that my place of birth is Hawaii. I was raised in Orange County, California. 1985. For the first time in my life, I escorted my mother to visit the homeland of both my mother and father who grew up there.

My Samoan language apparently was tainted with an American accent to the point where, when I spoke it in the homeland public, the locals laughed and mocked how I was speaking. I understood what they were saying, which was "Ole tama lea o'le fia palangi."

I recall being in my twenties and the fact that I was being mocked by locals of my own culture that I loved put me in a mental and emotional place that I now no longer wanted to speak to or being seen in the motherland as Samoan.

Gratefully, I moved past this experience because I learned their perspective was theirs. Not to mention back in the 1960s, 70s, and 80s, not too many homegrown Samoans ever get the chance to leave Samoa and visit other overseas places like America.

I know that back at this time, it was my grandparents' and parents' generation. In my generation, it was not as common being a first-generation American citizen for the past three generations living in the motherland, to travel stateside. The older generation does not speak English at all.

Today, I have learned through my experiential truths the facts that still my culture is tainted with divisions of Samoans not born or raised in the homeland. I experienced it when I met many who have now moved to America and yet still speak and live the culture as if they were still living on the islands.

Negative Karma

Ironically, I see the same thing come around now from Polynesians who were born and raised off-island in America, New Zealand, Australia, or whatever countries other non-English speaking Polynesians who moved to these countries.

Truth be told, I did it as well. I used the derogative connotation, calling these new nonspeaking Polynesians FOB short for (fresh off the boat.) However, after my experience in Samoa, I no longer do it by telling these new Polynesians that they are fobs.

Fear of losing tradition

The Polynesian cultures all have their versions of Lei's. Like the Hawaiian flower, Lei represents a circle of never-ending love, respect, and commitment. With a deep sense of pride, the Polynesian people maintain a rich and thriving culture. Exemplifying language, dances, love, respect, and commitment.

In the isle's homeland, children are taught the culture, family unity, love, respect, sharing and obedience.

When you move off the island and engage more in the American lifestyle, it is easy to lose their culture. Especially when free agency is given and other multi-cultures are the majority, it is easy to veer away from one's cultural teachings.

I feel that the effects of when and where you were born as a Polynesian should not matter. Nevertheless, the reality is that the answer to this question can vary depending on where and from whom you seek it, particularly across different generations. Let me offer my insights on generational topics from the standpoint of being a baby boomer with a diverse background of Samoan/Tongan, Chinese, and Scottish heritage.

Priced out of Paradise

A mainstay issue for Polynesians such as Hawaiians is the fact that the United States occupies Hawaii nei.

Dr. Sid, what are you saying or implying?

It is a sad reality that the greed of those in positions of power hinders native Hawaiians from being able to afford a place they can truly call their own. I was born in Hawaii, but I am not a Hawaiian, I am Samoan by culture.

The fact that anywhere on the islands that it is overrun by non-Hawaiian politicians who are wielding the lives of the indigenous natives such as the Hawaiians seems to be ok with making things hard.

Homes, vehicles, food, gas... you name it is too expensive for any family to afford to live in paradise just on one working salary. Sadly, in the democratic states, especially the state of Hawaii, which is the most unfordable state to live in and buy a house, taxes are extremely high; inflation increases monthly and an average family of four in 2023 pays about 2250 dollars a month for a two-bedroom apartment.

Truth be told, many politicians of all parties in Hawaii have contributed to making Hawaii and the local natives priced out of paradise. Still, only 30 percent of native-born Hawaiians own a home on the homestead, which is a US federally protected land for the indigenous Hawaiians who have 50 percent Hawaiian blood.

Sadly, the waiting list is long and many people from the silent era and the baby boomer generation have been waiting for over three decades to receive homestead land.

Chapter 5

LESSONS FROM ADAM AND EVE ON HUMAN IMPROVEMENT

How did Adam and Eve intersect to make us better humans?

We know what happened to Adam and Eve. Our understanding is that Eve was beguiled by the serpent. We saw the results. The takeaway is that we can hopefully learn from others' mistakes. However, for most, we must learn the hard way through only experiencing challenges, trials, and tribulations.

Today's version of the Tree of Knowledge is being played out openly on social media internet on our millennials and Z-generation. Our youth are innocent, naïve, and inexperienced.

Being inundated, addicted, and lured to social media platforms causes catastrophic consequences of being cast out of the garden.

The evil social media seed of addictions results in catastrophic ways when the guidance of God is not in their lives. No direction and no boundaries lead to addictions, peer pressure, pride, blame, and the results of mental health issues of anxiety, stress, and depression disorder.

Disconnect from family, friends, and community. Why do we blame others? Why do we feel we have no purpose in life? Feeling worthless. No direction. No goals. No control. Hatred. Suicide.

> ***Teach our children through example; direction is better than speed. Guide them to understand life's challenges and consequences.***

The Tree of Knowledge

While placed in the Garden of Eden, Adam and Eve were innocent, naïve, and inexperienced. They were allowed to partake of all the fruits from every tree in the garden, except one, the fruit from the tree of knowledge of good and evil.

God had given two commandments: first to multiply and replenish the earth, and second, to not partake of the fruit from the tree of knowledge of good and evil. They were given free agency to choose to obey God's commandments or not.

The outcome was that Eve chose to partake of the fruit of good and evil after being beguiled by the serpent (Satan). The second decision was made by Adam, who broke the first commandment to live the second commandment, which was to multiply and replenish the earth. Adam needed to be with Eve.

The takeaway from seeing what can happen is being seen today from our latest generation of disobedience. God showed us he loves us through his commandments and offering us a way to repent and be renewed through his son, Jesus Christ, who atoned for us all.

If we do not follow God's commandments and teach our children to keep within boundaries, they will fail on their own accord of not having been given boundaries, and suffer harsh consequences. **The result is that we learn through challenges, trials, and tribulations.**

Progression over mistakes comes when we understand and realize the consequent results. Understanding these types of harsh learning experiences has three types of result paths. First, God and adversary sent. Second, self-inflicted, and third, others free agency.

Regardless of how we experience challenges, trials, and tribulations the takeaway of learning is according to our ability to comprehend little by little, line upon line, and precept upon precept. Now imagine how hard it is for the youths to have nonstop challenges while in their innocent, naïve, and inexperienced mental state.

"We need to teach our children and the youth through our examples. Start life slowly, for direction is better than speed."

Maybe teach them exercises on real-life situations to work through and share the harsh consequences before they experience them in life. However, for parents and guardians, there is no better truth and lessons in life than experiencing life's pros and cons.

Chapter 6

INSTITUTIONAL RACISM, DISCRIMINATION, AND DIVISION

Racism, is it institutionalized?

Through past generations, our great grandparents to our parents have fought in their time and generation for the future of their offspring so racism would or would not be our fight today.

Currently today, we have progressed through racism for minorities such that it is noted that an African American president, African vice president, top generals of military branches, and in over 80 percent of top journalism television stations (i.e.) NBC. ABC, CBS, FOX, CNN, you will see minority faces as a normality.

Does this mean racism is over? Absolutely not even close. Sadly, racism and prejudices, in my opinion, will always be around as a mechanism to blame regardless of what race, gender, sex, age, or beliefs are in charge. Truly, racism is anchored in the facts of life that there is an opposition in all things.

The word racism as defined by Webster: rac.ism [ˈrāˌsizəm]

NOUN

prejudice, discrimination, or antagonism by an individual, community, or institution against a person or people on the basis of their membership in a particular racial or ethnic group, typically one that is a minority or marginalized:

"a program to combat racism,"

the belief that different races possess distinct characteristics, abilities, or qualities, especially so as to distinguish them as inferior or superior to one another.

As a minority from the baby boomer generation, I will go with the experiences I have had and my understanding of the layout of a certain culture of people's views that this is absolutely an individual or community-based prejudice from past offenses against minorities and not institutionalized across the nation.

I have to say as a Polynesian with brown skin; I recall small talks with older family members and friends who talked about racism experiences in their lives. Now that I know what racism is, I too have experiences of racism.

My takeaway regarding racism is that people do not cope well with things that are different.

The change in what people see that is different compared to what they normally are used to seeing is what makes people nervous, scared, or afraid of what the results may be.

Afraid of change they will have to deal with people who look different, talk differently, act differently, believe differently, think, and feel differently.

Being different does weird things to people who act out or speak out through being mistreated, taunted, ridiculed, gossiped, and shamed.

People who see others as different somehow act out to protect themselves regardless of not being mistreated. I call it what it is, racial profiling.

I know one thing, that's a fact. In a world of multiple cultures, we as a human society need to develop thick skin for different races, colors, genders, beliefs, dress, and culture.

Sadly, some people do not want to see change and when they bring about the thought of change to their immediate surroundings, they do not care whose feelings they hurt.

The good thing regarding those who are racist is that **we can choose to be offended or choose to help break the stereotype of being different by making others feel comfortable** regarding our different looks, language, beliefs, and cultures.

If we act upon the ignorance of other people by being offended ourselves, we inadvertently become part of that same ignorance. When it comes to change, it has to be seen both ways.

If we do not extend our humanitarian hand of friendship, then we are no better at seeing people who also look, act, and speak differently from us. Therefore, are we not doing the same thing? This will be our downfall as a society and humanitarian generation.

> *"Racism arises from fear of differences; overcoming it requires empathy, tolerance, and understanding.*

Modern-Day Culture

In generation gaps, we do not take into consideration the effects of eight hours of schooling away from home and our family that affects our psyche, not to mention living in another country surrounded by multiple cultures.

In the past generation of the 1970s to 1990s, million-dollar grossing revenue could be found at arcade locations in the city where kids used to meet, hang out, and play video games, especially after school and on weekends.

Today, as never before seen, these million-dollar video technology gaming supply and demand companies have kicked into billion-dollar corporations, constantly morphing into advanced digital state-of-the-art game-producing companies. These companies began offering home setting play station controls and devices, which morphed into powerhouse companies such as Play Stations, Microsoft, Command and Conquer, and even Sony.

The video games of the past such as Pacman, Donkey Kong, Galaga, and Mario have changed and are considered a relic of the past. The second-generation video games took a whole new direction, such as Mortal Kombat, Tomb Raider, and Command and Conquer, in which I played characters through motion capture.

First, video games went from analog-to-digital. Second, the digital games came with backline storylines. Some games were pitched from movies to video games. Anyway, to generate a profit and these strategic movies to video games panned out big time, these movie projects changed the mindsets of my generation of the Baby Boomers and X-generation. A few of these video games are Mortal Kombat, Street Fighter, Sniper, Halo, Tomb Raider, Resident Evil, etc.

This is a billion-dollar supply and demand company that seems to do its job and keep the players' minds involved. These mind-altering up-grade digital video games have again morphed into advanced technology into the future of now playing games with controllers that react to your movements, wireless hand-held devices, and listen to your voice commands. Indeed, these games have changed and have stayed considerably digitally advanced and relevant.

Today's games have morphed again for the Millennials, Z-Generation, and Alpha generations. At a time with past generations where teens used to play games as a mental fantasy escape or mental getaway.

If you can understand, this is considered modern-day 'P&Q' as we share in our generation, aka 'peace and quiet'. During this period, Millennials and Gen-Z are afflicted with anxiety, stress, and depression due to the various generational changes. Such generations grow up watching their parents, guardians, and grandparents overwork themselves in order to maintain what they have or what they want. These young generations want to avoid it, which is why gaming is huge.

These games that include superheroes and various characters played on these updated digital video games have now morphed into fantasy characters that include costumes and characters. These gatherings mainly happen in the United States such as com-i-con, and magic fantasy conventions by thousands of young generation attendees.

Today, there are huge conventions in which these Millennials, Gen-Z, and Alpha pay a good sum of money not only to attend but come dressed up as their game character heroes made costumes which is a big annual showing at the Las Vegas Convention Center attendees.

Las Vegas Convention Visitor Authority welcomes Millennials and Z-Generation by the thousand-stand inline.

People dress up as their favorite game characters and enter their costume pageant.

Committed video games stood in long lines, enjoyed the gaming competitions, dressed in costumes, and walked around outside in the hot 108-degree regardless of temperature.

From life to video games, when is fantasy culture too much?

Even when the weatherman issues a severe hot weather warning, it is not enough to bring these gamers out of full costume characters. These convention attendees are hardcore lifers.

I see the future generations. If they do not have boundaries and continue in the same fashion, they will be exposing their future kids to unwanted dangers and addictions in the name of 'this is who I am as a character.'

For these Millennials and Gen-Z generations, it does not matter whether it's race, ethnicity, or video game costumes, they see no difference in cultures.

The High Chief's decisions of the past do not answer the issues of the present or the future.

Our Polynesian traditions of love, respect, and culture have been set. However, the influences on our next generations are constantly changing and affecting the culture with new perspectives. Including a first-time global pandemic change that affected the entire globe and Samoan islands and our families.

The common villagers, especially our youth, have never had a voice in the past to speak or persuade their issues or grievances to the talking chiefs and or high chief because of the traditional protocol of respect and culture.

The Resolve

The Culture of 'Aiga' or family, love, and respect is set and does not and will not change. However, when influential changes occur in the culture, the protocols also need to adapt and change according to the issues or crisis.

The resolve can be protocol changes during epic times when the entire island is affected, let us say, by a virus disease, or drug outbreak that affects all. Only these periods should the Matai's or high chiefs allow the commoners and youth voices to be heard to speak their truth, illness, or grievances directly to them as a community of what they are experiencing as decisions are being made.

Ironically, today in various countries where other Samoans off-island reside who are still affected by the pandemic during these times, no flights were allowed in or out to the island nations, yet the leadership can still change and communicate through technology of Facebook Live or zoom, etc.

The great thing about today's computer technology is that the younger generations, by a higher percentage, are already more advanced in this usage due to their generation environment.

If the culture is to survive the next generations, regardless of technology or not, the high chiefs must include the leadership of the next generations. By communicating with the next generation through listening to learn, then learning to listen, lifting them to higher cultural expectations.

Do Design Flaws Exist?

I am sure centuries ago, there were flaws when the Matai status was passed on from father to son. It was a great honor.

I am sure back in centuries past, not having a son rather a daughter must have been considered a flaw or disappointment not able to continue the male chief bloodline of who thought only their male gender could appease and hold the mana or power recognized by 'Tetua' God.

Based on my personal experiences, I have learned that it is possible to be born into a certain family with a specific culture and become a natural blood brother or sister.

What life has not taught until the late century is that we find people in our lives that are not related by blood but are closer to us, as trusted to us and just as loving as a father or mother, brother, sister or cousin to you.

Polynesian culture can be a birthright of expectation; however, its tradition, belief, or culture seemingly can be and has been adopted by countless non-Polynesians. However, live the Polynesian lifestyle of traditions, language, and culture, and surprisingly, one would not be able to tell they were not Polynesian by blood.

> ***In a diverse society, we must develop thick skin and compassion to bridge gaps between cultures and generations.***

What Does a Win look like?

At the end of the day. I live and love my unique Polynesian culture, as well as cultures period.

If other non-Polynesians find that living in our culture speaking our languages, eating our foods puts a smile on their faces and enjoys living it, then I support them or you one hundred percent.

To each our own of whatever makes us happy.

So as a Polynesian, American, or a member of my latter-day saint faith, whether I feel, or whether someone else feels a certain way, it does not matter.

At the End of the Day what matters is how you feel and what makes you happy.

I have seen Polynesians hesitant, murmur, or get upset about other non-Polynesians engaging in our Polynesian cultures because they, as Polynesians, are very proud of their culture and do not want to see it mocked.

If a non-Polynesian person steps over the line of trying to change the culture or presents it incorrectly or in a bad light, they should be corrected by a Polynesian and yes, that includes me.

If non-Polynesians who adapt to our culture and they incidentally try yet do not fully understand our culture, they will be corrected but not in a harsh firm manner. Understanding all cultures is a lifestyle that is sustained by love, pride, protocols, language, and tradition.

Now that said, there are those who, just because it's in their normal habit of life, are negative of anything having to do with culture. In life, they are like crabs in a bucket. If one crab tries to crawl out of the bucket, other crabs will pull the crab back down into the bucket. I express it as a metaphor that can be used when people in life are jealous, angry, or envious of others all the time.

The reality is that not all are Polynesians or non-Polynesians for that fact. We're taught love, respect, support, and serving others. These are civility-type attributes that are deeply engrained in our culture.

If non-Polynesians embrace our culture and share our culture with others in places of the world representing the culture in a manner that we Polynesians would have other non-Polynesians learn and or embrace our culture, we are greatly honored and from my perspective of having someone share your culture in honor, pride, and love; to me, that is absolutely a win-win.

I use the words to relate to my culture that I love.

"In general, law, life, and limb must be protected but often a limb may be amputated to save a life, but never a life is given to save a limb." **-Abraham Lincoln**

Fortified by Generational Philosophy Inclusion.

Imagine the past (older) generation's parental upbringing for disciplining their children where they would not allow their child or children's voice to be heard while the parents were disciplining them or physically spanking them as punishment.

Respect always seems to be the bottom line. When parents discipline their child or children regarding any issue, it boils down to respecting their parent(s). For so many generations, the child or the children were not allowed to speak their grievances.

Nope. During the greatest generation, the silent generation, or Korean GI generation disciplined was served with children keeping their mouths shut while the parents seemed to know better what they were doing.

Sadly, as the following generation learned, all they did was learn to continue to continue the punishments.

Today, imagine the 21st century generation where parental discipline and physical punishment is considered an abuse and or against the law. Apparently, in this millennial or Z-generation, discipline has totally changed to almost no (public) physical punishment.

To be or not to be... like Mom and Dad

Work, work, work.

Just the thought, when dad, mom, or guardian mention their work ethics to be financially successful, it is a downer. For this younger generation, work is a bust and it puts pressure on them.

Even when parents are business owners or employed by a great company, Millennials and Gen-z children oppose to live by the philosophy of their parent's expectation for them.

'Monkey See Monkey Do' situation.

Millennials and Gen-z know that at some point, they must get jobs or start a business. Of course, dad and mom are working to provide the blueprint that will fashion the same successful results.

For Millennials and gen-z, this comparison stresses and freaks them out. This can be depressing when most children do not want to be like their parents, working at something they hate, spending all their time away sacrificing for the family.

Millennials and gen-z dislike the comparison parents make between their sacrificial work ethics and their expectation for their children regarding work.

Almost without an option, parents expect their children to do the same thing so they can be independent and financially stable. The young generation have a negative view of following their parent's employment footsteps.

Most Millennials and gen-z would rather opt for their desired career. A considerable percentage consists of gamers. The parents do not understand gamers and absolutely feel it is a waste of time playing video games.

The issue is during the parent's timeline as baby boomers and generation-X, it really was just playing video games. Today the younger generation of gamers can make a living from being professional gamers. The gaming industry is a billion-dollar business. Today gamers can make money. There are players who get paid millions of dollars as a result of their skills in gaming.

Another main contributing factor that fills Millennials and gen-z with negativity is the social media platforms. Social media is a false and misleading platform of how they can live a purposeful and successful life.

Today's social media platform is about selling fantasy to the younger generation who do not understand the consequences until it's too late. The young, naive and innocent minds are devastated and stressed when they expect life to be easy but it turns out to be hard. The irony about challenges, trials, and tribulations is that it becomes your experience of truth. Now you know.

Chapter 7

CULTURAL IMPACTS AT HOME

Home Impact of Cultures With-In Cultures (Politics)

Dr. Sid Liufau. My parents were raised in the Samoan Islands, then moved to Hawaii in the 1960s where I and my sister were born. First-generation American citizens. 1973 we moved to Orange County, California. I was raised with a strong Christian and Polynesian cultured background.

Santa Ana, California, was another place of my growing-up years. In my family, I grew up there without a father. My mother was both parents who worked several jobs, so I hardly saw her. However, we had six siblings living in the house. My mother had sent word to her brother living in Samoa she needed help. He came to live with us; as kids, we called him the uncle from hell.

This uncle single-handedly took away our freedom by forcing us to learn self-defense in our garage directly after we got home from school and finished our homework. For five years straight, the five of us siblings had to show up three hours a day, for six days a week.

The only exception to missing self-defense class was if we were sick or dead. He would make sure we made up for missing days.

I despised this uncle who lacked compassion. We all regretted that he ever came to live with us. He instilled such a profound fear in us that it was truly overwhelming. We felt like slaves every day to his every demand. Even our mother said nothing to him when he would beat or punish us. I grew up angry that we were denied our youth years of enjoying ourselves hanging out with our school or neighborhood friends.

After seven years when my mother remarried, he finally moved back to the islands, **but it was too late because the damage kids was already done.** What does that mean? It means my truth was locked in on what someone else's forced truth did to become my truth because it was a method I would never agree to support or use and by all powers of mine makes sure it does not get planted or entangled even by accident in my teaching of acceptability to my posterity.

This experience of feeling like slaves and having no choice left a negative seed of depression. Sadly, it came back again into fruition, affected and related to political realms through the support of legislations that give no choices to us as American citizens, instead passed as federal mandatories.

> *"Strict upbringing taught me resilience, but community programs were my saving grace, proving the crucial role of government support in youth development.*

City or Generational Impact

I also recall mostly being surrounded by political democrats who influenced our communities and relied on government funding for youth programs.

Growing up in our schools, work or even political ethnicity were mostly led by Caucasians. Through the years that followed, a heavy influence of minorities got involved in the political community outreach. Cities like Santa Ana, Garden Grove, and Westminster were mainly filled with minority families who lived, played, living, and participated in city programs.

In Santa Ana, I recall two community youth centers; Corbin center and Jerome Center. These two nonprofit organizations focused on youths like me, providing programs that helped and inspired youths with hope. Gratefully, there was government funding that allowed these centers to prove sports programs.

These nonprofit organizations for countless youths helped us focus on positive things rather than having us stay idle or get ourselves into trouble.

I hope this allows you, the reader, the ability to relate better as to what my truth and influences were while growing up. As a minority, these programs assisted countless youths and teens like me, especially coming from low-income single parents raising seven children.

Regardless of having two parents or being raised by a single mother, if the parents worked continuously, the emotional support suffered. However, family circumstances and community leaders partnered with government finances were the bridge for kids to find support and were indeed my saving grace of opportunities.

There's a saying "That idleness is the playground of the devil". Because of past experiences and my family's positive experiences, I give back what has been given to me.

That said, many of these nonprofit organizations and private youth entities need to be sustained through government funding and subsidies. Politics plays a huge role in funding city programs and making things happen.

Life Choice Impact?

First, I began by sharing my youth upbringing through the grace of the Almighty God.

Second, I recognize the influences and actions of community leaders who exemplify civility on how they lived through serving others, creating hope and joy.

Third, I state as a fact when I first heard Dr. Clyde Rivers speak in 2019, over three-four years ago. His message and actions reminded me of my youth hood tutelage that was placed in my path that created hope and joy through his service.

Dr. Rivers, till today, exemplifies and inspires through his Civility-based truths that immediately cause one to not only listen, but to want to learn and engage.

I attest through his profound civility tools of humanity that interrupt the stalled narratives of which behooves me and changes for the betterment of contributing peace in the public square.

I prepped a topic for this segment which, seemingly for most, the internal workings are unknown.

Chapter 8

INTRA POLITICS

First, as a baby boomer generation growing up, there were two specific topics I was always told in general to stay away from when others engage in conversation, religion, and politics.

With that being said, it is highly likely that I will touch on both subjects to some extent.

This past 2022 Presidential election, I am sure the world can agree that it was and still currently is today (2/1/2023) a hot mess.

Now I will cut to the chase. I do not care whether you are a Democrat, Republican or Independent. I do not even care what your religion or faith is.

No, rather my focus is on two different perspectives.

Number One, political intentions of candidate's verses promise made, and promises kept.

Number Two, as an American citizen, what rights do you have in changing the Global Humanitarian conditions that affect all?

In the past, the norms regarding American political affairs were taken serious and well respected.

Sadly, today, American political affairs are seen as corrupt and fraudulent.

When political candidates campaign, they usually make promises that if given the opportunity, they will change the negative situation to a positive status in any political office of corrupt officials whether in the Federal, State, County, City, or from the Governments highest office to the lowest elected positions.

Today, the word 'politics' has earned a deserving to negative connotation and negative additives that includes past, present, and future candidates, and their promises that they have, do and will make which normally ends up mocked by the phrase "Lair-lair pants on fire".

Far too often, during these political periods of campaigning for governmental elections, we the people hoped to see a change in the issues of needed topics such as negative economic and hardships.

We, the American people, have become experts at watching and listening to politicians campaigning on negative topics, promising that if elected, to expect to see a change that he or she will make. Sadly, we have witnessed time and time again as the norms of the disappointments the candidates show once get elected to office. The reality is that they seem to get hit by a bad medical memory case of amnesia of loss promises.

Unfortunately, it seems like it does not matter who is in office as the results of unkept promises the expected results in the political world is that if change does not occur, we can try again in another election.

As a loving and supportive father of five wonderful children and five grandchildren. I have coached, watched, and enjoyed all my children in after-school sports. Lastly, my youngest and only boy Teyvin-Justice has engaged in 8-11 years old flag football.

Teyvin began playing and in his first seasonal flag football, it was all about learning and understanding the game. He earned a reputation as a defensive rusher and running down the quarterback. The second season, he learned and adapted to offense with a keen ability to hone in his running back talents.

Teyvin's running back skills became noticeably averaging two touchdowns a game. His unpredictable ability to run one direction and as his opponents gave chase, he suddenly would cut back, changing direction and using the described word "Juke!" Teyvin juking skills built his confidence as a running back and my earned title the Juking King.

As an expert in observing political lie after lie, I noticed a comparison to my son's football ability to juke and politicians increasing confidence abilities to do the same and Juke the American people with unfilled promises.

Yes, politicians have the same abilities to have their supporters think when they made promises they would keep them and that they would bring change. However, once they got elected, the politicians would do the old 'Juke move' and not keep their promises.

In my truth, it would be wise if all citizens learn to understand the gravity of what's at stake once politicians get elected.

Political Mockery

However, after becoming an expert in political movements and mostly all candidates juke once they get elected, unfortunately are a little more complex than just unkept promises of lies.

Again, as an expert observer, I believe there are sensible reasons most politicians learn deception through negotiations. It is because they are forced to preserve their own lives. Dr. Sid, what are you talking about?

Let me explain, the art of negotiation comes right out of the 'Art of War' play book. This book was written by Sun Tzu in the 1500s by a warlord.

It encompasses the perfect strategy to pretend as you strengthen your political foundation to survive. One of Sun Tzu's famous philosophies and saying is 'keep your friends close and your enemies closer.'

This strategy is a good one, regardless of it being a mockery of promises made. The value for politicians is to use and get information? Know the enemy's weakness. Another strategy is to 'know when to fight, and know when not to fight.'

At times, military strategy tricks to employ this type of weak foot forward to entice their enemies to attack is a strategy to be seen and thought of as weak enemies. A military method of war used to take advantage of an already position offensive counter strike is to sacrifice less of your warriors to destroy more of the enemies.

There are many strategies; however, one of the most used strategies by the senior politicians is to be aggressive to survive. This is done by controlling and making the rules. Aggressive negotiating by controlling the newly elected politicians by threatening them to join a team rather than be solo, and this is regardless of political parties, these strategies are used to keep control.

The point is senior or career politician who has had longevity in this industry knows how to negotiate. This control bait to get the newbie politician to support whatever the career senior caucus majority want is normally the results.

The threats to make the newly elected politicians play along in the sandbox or find themselves (soloist) as a one term politician out of the box with no voice and no support.

These actions will result in the newbie fizzling out and regardless of the people who elected them to have represented them to be their voice. It's a totally unfamiliar power play. It is a rare occurrence for citizens to acknowledge their own tendencies towards using bullying tactics and acting above the law.

If I were to use the comparison of being in prison. In prison, the thought of fair justice or rules to follow is absurd. For those serving life terms from being hardened, felonies operate and are likely the ones in charge of the prisons.

Sadly, the warden and the guards only run the administrative system side. Sorry to tell you, but the warden and guards do not control the prison lifers. These lifers have created a prison system that gives them control.

Consider the correlation. The warden and guards are like the federal government. Prisoners are like career lifers and gangs, they're like the state law enforcement. (They make the rules because they run the prison.)

Although criminals get sentence and the warden determine who and what cell. It's the state career lifer and gang inmates who control the prisons. Criminals come and go for a shorter time, but they must live according to the state's controllers. (Career lifer or gang leaders.)

The difference of perspective, the guards work in prison, the career inmates live in prison. Their mindsets are that there is nothing you can do to them that will change their outcome.

Now the guards will tell you at the end of the day, they leave to go home to their families. The prisoners have made their new home and their new families in prison.

> *As a baby boomer, I've seen political promises come and go, often unfulfilled. We must hold leaders accountable and stand for integrity, or risk falling for anything.*

Political Corruption System

As an American citizen and individual, our political system in 2023 is so corrupt and polluted with fraud, deception, and malice. That includes political power that weaponize branches of government to do their dirty work of investigation against opponents or hide fraud by not arresting the criminals.

The blatant political power play and weaponizing government branches are blanketed with injustice and hypocrisy. This is done to keep power and continue to engage in wealthy scams hidden in scrupulous legislative laws.

It is no wonder why we see the juke moves very often being used by elected politicians and career politicians once they get into office. Like prison, either they put up with the corruption by turning a blind eye to get along and accept the corrupt bully tactics or they turn away and find themselves all alone with no support as a one term politician and an easy target to take out.

American Election Voters

Now, as for the average citizens who talk like they know everything; we already know during the elections and political campaigning, we have typical three types of citizens:

One who watches the elections.

One who talks about the elections.

One who engages in the elections.

That said, by all rights and standards as citizens, we have every right to be any type of these citizens. I will also point out that I have been all three types of citizens during my lifetime.

Dr. Sid, what is the point?

When it comes to anything in life, talk is cheap, seeing is believing, especially when it involves political candidates and what they say and what they do. As a baby boomer generation, my stance is clear: "Either you put up or shut up." Because for us and keeping these politicians accountable for choices that will affect our lives and our families, "Either you stand for something good, or you will fall for anything bad."

When family, friends or people in general start talking to me about politics and religion specially with people I do not know, I try very hard to stay away from the two topics of conversations that will cause clash and animosity, especially when the past acts of politicians come into play.

Example: Today, if you talk about supporting President Donald J Trump, you're already labeled a lair, Russian spy, racist, sexist, radical MAGA patriot radical.

If you supported President Joseph Biden, you're labeled a lair, Chinese-owned, sick with dementia, a child's hair sniffer, or Obama's lap dog.

In the now, I am comfortable to engage any topic that I have firsthand knowledge of information. I try to get the information directly from my spiritual source.

So, when I hear politically correlated buzz words that I know from the mainstream media source that may be true or not true, sadly, it will always include negative dialogue from the opposing side. Unfortunately, like most people during elections, they harbor negative feelings towards the candidate's speeches and acts of their past.

In the past, I have seemed to be like the most disappointed voting citizen focus and concerned about negative things I hear from candidates who like to bash and be condescending.

In proverbs, we are reminded that our tongues have the ability to speak life or death.

In the New Testament found in Galatians, we learn that "by their fruits ye shall you know."

You can bet that 80 percent of people (citizens) who vote for candidates do not really know much about the candidate's real intentions.

As a society, we have become jaded by the party label, which, sadly, is a waste of time because it causes negativity. Many sides on listening to the mainstream news media outlets as dependable sources, which again sadly has become politicized with misinformation from the past.

2022-2023, today's clear political battle is the Republic verses Democracy.

re·pub·lic

1. A state in which supreme power is held by the people and their elected representatives, and which has an elected or nominated president rather than a monarch.

- A group with a certain equality between its members:

de·moc·ra·cy

2. A system of government by the whole population or all the eligible members of a state, typically through elected representatives:

- control of an organization or group by most of its members:

The Political Judging

At this point in my life, I live in the now, which means I will continue to change political parties if my views and their views conflict in belief. The parties have changed their stances and so I have changed parties due to it.

Again, the point I hope I made is whether or not you agree with someone's politics, whether you feel it is your duty to have a voice against corruption, or not. If you are going to take a moral stance on fortitude, then equally call corruption regardless of where it comes from. The phrase is simply to call a spade a spade, regardless of who it affects and how it makes them look.

I can relate to something that I did negatively that changed my life, which affected my wife. Although my negative behavior may have never come to suffer, nevertheless, I never attempted to hide my negative actions from my wife.

The way my mind is wired is regardless of the good or bad, especially bad whether it does or it comes to suffice my belief is that I know, and

I know God knows I did something wrong and need to confess and repent or it will come out on judgement day so why try to hide it.

I would rather be a person who is seen for my wrong trespasses, repent, reproved and pay restitution rather than going to my grave as a silent liar hiding my lies with more lies.

Although I do not agree with many political views on how some of the way politicians handle things in secret, I still hope for the best that they find integrity to resolve their trespasses. I hope we still feel that we can give politicians the opportunities to make amends and or deliver their promises to the American people and move on instead harp on negative banter and waste time.

The truth is that the grave is full of good intentions. So, what profits a person who never does the things he or she should, promises and the other things out of fear? The fear of failing. The fear of committing. Having an attitude anchor should be an automatic daily mindset to which our mental and spiritual foundation is anchored on.

For example, why get involved in anything such as a simple conversation unless we can contribute to being better candidates or citizens or being a better person? Why trample down a negative road that leads to negative conversation?

We need to understand what may be true for you, what may not be true for me, and vice versa. Truth pros and cons is the journey as experienced and resulted for the individual, which becomes a real and true, experienced outcome.

Parents may teach their children what the parents want their children to know and learn, but if the child is not ready to know, learn or especially experience such teachings, what the parents teach them will never be the child's truth.

Instead, it will be sprinkled seeds for the planting in the child's mind. The growth of the seeds comes when the child is able and ready to want to know and understand the point of the parent's truth.

I shared earlier in my growing years how my uncle forced us to live a certain expectation all in the name of knowing what's best for us kids.

When the coronavirus pandemic hit us and we were forced to wear masks, forced to stay home, forced to stay distanced, forced to receive the coronavirus injection to keep our jobs.

Through my experiences as a child of having no say and now again as an adult, these forced mandates only cause me to think negatively about what were these politicians thinking when they passed the law to mandate people's freedom. Politically wise I do not care what political party you are with in my truth. If you take away any chance to allow me to choose, I will not be supporting that person or that political party that supports any ideology of mandates.

We all have different mindsets and truths which I think are wonderful. The minute you cancel my truth, I will do the same to you.

In short, who gives 'anyone' the right to cancel your truth? You may not agree and that's ok. You may not support and that's ok. But you have no right to tell me, or I also have no right to tell you that your truth is wrong.

> ***Navigating politics today is like watching a football game; politicians often 'juke' the public with unkept promises. We need to anchor ourselves in truth and resilience, striving for a higher standard of integrity and responsibility.***

Pride of Political Greed gets to judge others

In 2022, a recent finding of illegal donations to Dems and GOP showed a new frontier of influences.

Before his arrest, Bankman-Fried had embarked on a media tour to sway public opinion and control the narrative. In the interviews, he explained how the overnight implosion of his empire was because of bad luck. “I made a lot of mistakes,” he said during his first interview on Nov. 30 with The New York Times/Deal Book. “There are things I would give anything to do over again. I never tried to commit a fraud on anyone.”

Bankman-Fried had become the institutional face of crypto, spending most of his time in Washington, where he tried to influence the direction of the young industry's regulation. He consequently contributed millions of dollars to elect Democrats. The former trader emerged as a major donor to Democratic candidates, leading up to the Nov. 8 midterm elections.

His political action committee gave over $23 million to the Democratic Party while the 30-year-old founder of FTX gave $13 million of his own money to both the Democrats and Republicans, according to filings with the Federal Election Commission. But executives of FTX and its American subsidiary, FTX US, were making donations to Republicans.

On Oct. 27, 2022, twelve days before the midterm elections, FTX US donated $1 million to the Senate Leadership Fund Super-PAC, according to a filing with the FEC. The Super-PAC, which is lined up with Senate Minority Leader Mitch McConnell (R-Kentucky), says it "has one goal: to build a Republican Senate majority that will defend America from Chuck Schumer and Senate Democrats' destructive far-left agenda."

The donation was made by West Realm Shires Services, which is the trading name of FTX US.

FTX US also gave $750,000 to the Congressional Leadership Fund and $150,000 to the American Patriots PAC. The two PACs backed House Republican candidates. It also donated $100,000 to the Alabama Conservatives Fund.

Ryan Salame, the co-CEO of FTX Digital Markets, one of FTX's affiliates, donated nearly $24 million to the Republican Party, the records show. These donations were made amid growing calls for strict regulation of the crypto industry.

I share this not as a political look of who is saying what but because both republican and democratic politicians are doing things for themselves, not for the American people. Regardless of what we hear, watch the results of these politicians' actions. Many say things they did but really do to help the American citizens.

An attitude anchor should always be positive regardless of the circumstances. We need to strive for a standard of higher value in understanding, development, integrity, responsibility, trust, loyalty, dependability, and self-reliance.

Another prideful issue is I had to take a hiatus from film and television due to lack of projects, living in Las Vegas and not financially set.

Auditioning during the housing market crash inflation was hurting the economy and all of us. Driving back and forth to and from Las Vegas to Los Angeles was expensive. Gas was $5 a gallon at the time. It cost just as much for a round-trip plane ticket than to fill my minivan gas tank.

A maintenance anchor should be the mindset that allows one to be anchored in positive thoughts, vibes, and energy regardless of the negative surrounding oneself, even when offended. Philippians 4:8 says, "Seek after truth, honesty, just, pure, lovely, virtue and praise."

For example, a coworker is constantly condescending toward you even after politely discussing the issue.

Unless I feel what that person is saying is true, it doesn't affect me because I know the truth of who I am. One still has a choice to be offended and stay to the positive truth or be offended.

A repair anchor should be the mindset that helps us anchor past the damages and negative effects felt through our emotions and the mental and spiritual injuries caused or sustained by an act of God, by a person, or from a self-inflicted cause and effect.

Regardless of any past issues that linger, negativity is a poison. Having a repair mindset applied allows us to repair, reload, and recharge.

My hopes for you as you read my memoir is that you receive a rock-solid positive message that regardless of the challenges, trials, and tribulations in our lives, there is something possible, profound, and positive when a new perspective and attitude is gained.

The anchors are a foundation to be hopeful and positive through life's challenges, trials, and tribulations.

Chapter 9

HAPPINESS DEPENDENCE ON OTHERS LEADS TO DISAPPOINTMENT

Bottom line is, if we entrust our happiness to others, we will be disappointed.

If others can be fair, respectful, and courtesy, that's the best to ask.

When we trust our happiness in our belief, God and seeking the truth, we will never be disappointed.

Through extending the Golden rule "Treat others as you want to be treated." And the Golden question "If the shoe were on the other foot, would your decision be any different?"

Our belief in a higher power allows us to experience the light of goodness. I testify that the light of goodness brings happiness and fulfillment. So, regardless of being disappointed by politicians or whoever uses the method of Juking others with false promises.

I absolutely testify that by following and keeping God's commandments, our potential and eternal happiness will see the promises the God offers.

While going through challenges, trials, and tribulations of life's various levels, remember that most of the time, we will fall short. It is part of God's process and unless we humble ourselves to understand the bigger picture that we must depend on God and only he alone can give true eternal happiness be made known through the lord his son, Jesus Christ promises.

> "*True happiness comes from following God's commandments and treating others with fairness and respect, not from relying on others for our fulfillment.*

The Roles in the Year 2020 Seemingly have Changed in the Public Eye.

The parent almost does not have a voice in disciplining their children like past generations, regardless of if the child needs it due to being wrong.

A simple question, "Which of all generations raising children was the correct generation?"

Whatever discipline you use on your child or children will always be subjected to change. And regardless of the child, adult or anyone for that matter, discipline brings change, and no one enjoys being forced to change.

In fact, every generation of discipline or tradition comes as a two-edged sword. One side that cuts against one's truth, and the other side the cuts through your truth.

Parents from one generation and a child from a different generation will never be on the same page of understanding because it is two different generations: periods, environments, influences, experiences, etc.

The older generation comes with experiences of their learned truth. The younger generation comes with no experience and no understanding of consequences. Regardless, they may be taught something that is not taught with experiences of the big difference. In other words, the younger generation's truth is subjected to constant changes until they experience truth.

Ironically, the older generation is set in their ways, therefore, they feel their ways are correct and offer to teach the younger generation their truth.

The issue with that is even if the older generation has experiences, it may just be that they DO NOT have experiences (such as) in the new environment with advanced technology.

The new generation is beginning to experience harsh feelings on social media platforms, such as cyberbully.

Where other kids or people lash out negative condescending words at the younger generation, specifically calling out the youngster who has never experienced this before, and the person is totally humiliated and believes the lies being told that 'he or she is ugly and stupid as an example!'

Many youngsters do not understand an undeveloped mind also does not function correctly because for the young, naive mind to understand the consequences because they barely know the minimum of life. The bare minimum of understanding is dealing with no reasoning or logic who are greatly influenced and believe what they hear and follow through by taking their life.

This specific act or issue is the foundation of a war that has been going on since the world was created. This is most important to realize that this is 'a spiritual war of good versus evil.' It's aimed at the weak-minded and each generation the young, innocent, and naive does not understand this spiritual truth and the war that all God's children are being attacked and affected by the father of lies and disseverment by Lucifer or the devil.

Especially the innocent, naive, and inexperienced are who evil focuses on easily pursued and confused minds to get them to believe they are worthless.

Dr. Sid, what does that mean by two different generational truths?

Chapter 10

SELF-TRUST FOR FUTURE GENERATIONS

The Future Generation Have to Trust Oneself.

The Millennials, Generation-Z, Alpha, and Future Generations must get educated through research and experiential truths. As a baby boomer, I foresee these generations in trouble not being able to stand on their own. I see your generations are not just afraid of making hard decisions and just allowing the status quo to stand, not challenging anything, even though you know it is wrong.

I often stated when it comes to something relatable, **'if it walks like a duck, and quacks like a duck, then it's a duck!'**

The point is, if we are told specific things as an example that the roof is not on fire, yet we see with our eyes the roof is burning and black smoke billowing, I tend to believe what I see over what I am being told.

When it comes to people intentionally lying, they consider you are not smart enough to know the difference between truth and lies. This seems to have been going on for the past centuries by political parties.

And even though when these evil intentions continue to flat out lie to you because it does not matter. Why does it not matter to them? It's because it's not like you're going to do something about exposing the lies, anyway.

Dr. Suess shares a profound quote "Unless we are absolutely offended, the likelihood of things changing is not." This is true.

Millennials and Gen-Z, it's a high percentage that the perception of your generations that they do not care about lies and intentional nor misinformation. Though you may know the truth, you're too selfish to care about the outcome.

When absolute and intentional misinformation of wrong doings in the world is being enacted and the main news media or government narrative says that it is not what you think, I would absolutely call a duck a duck.

Most Millennials and Gen-Z do not care enough to fight the status quo and allow injustice to offend them. Seemingly, these generations would rather be like an Ostrich and bury their heads in the sand. I am sure you may need to look up this older past quote online (Hahaha).

However, hear this WARNING! If these generations do not stand up before the offenders take away your truths and power, you are going to lose the chance of living with freedom, liberty, and justice for all in their future.

You cannot be a fencing sitter. You must choose aside. Just going along with whatever the main news media or government tells you or someone says you should do just because they said so, sorry, but that will not suffice.

We Must Value Your Worth

You cannot stay in an environment where people do not know your true value. If you stay around those types of people, you will shrink your gifts to the size of what they can stand, to make you feel less than what your true worth is which makes one feel incompetent and of low self-esteem which is part of what causes anxiety, stress, and depression orders.

Do Not Assume, Listen and Verify

This is my opinion from what I researched to what I have seen, that the United States is headed down a path where the world's 1% of the wealthiest and influential people on earth seem to have been buying land, homes, and farms. They have been paying off the corrupt swamp governments to intervene in political influences, peddling government socialism, buying judges, lawyers, people of influences to change laws, rights, traditional cultures and force their evil ploy aimed to end human rights of freedom and choice. The plan is to have all nations and eventually, the American people under their dictated powers.

> ***Millennials and Gen-Z must rise above complacency, seek truth through research, and stand against misinformation to protect their freedoms and values.***

(A.I) Artificial Intelligence

A.I has already been used on social media to copy people's identity of looks facial recognition, speech, and mannerisms.

As a society, we believe in what our eyes tell us and what our ears hear; that becomes our truth.

Now, imagine if a software app can take and manipulate digital data of someone's looks and voice profile and download it to use as a fake video message pretending it was from the person whose digital information was stolen and sent to other family members to use to extort money from the family and loved ones.

Would you be shocked? Because that just happened for real.

In April 2023, the news media aired that a kidnapping had taken place. That a frantic mother was being extorted to send money, that kidnappers had taken her daughter.

The kidnappers aired the daughter's voice and mother panicked, trying to get the sum much money as quick as possible.

The family members heard the mother's commotion and raced to assist. One family member called the father, who was at work.

The father called the daughter directly on her phone and was confused when the daughter answered the phone.

Surprisingly, she was just fine and relaxing at her place. Unaware of the kidnapping event.

The father called the wife and shared the news not to send any money, instead call the police.

The police were notified, and the police IT department shared that what the criminals did was to use an (A.I) Artificial intelligence software app that was recently made available online.

Explaining that when engaged, it can copy people's digital profile, upload specific voice analyst, and video footage and compile them together to be used on social media and even make it look like you're saying something that you never said.

A.I is a smart generational software that, as it continues to evolve, may become even smarter and more dangerous in the wrong hands, including on its own.

Now you see what I see, which we would possibly believe is truth.

Chapter 11

EMBRACING RAPID CHANGE

Fast Changing is the Future?

In Mid-2022, Elon and two other billionaires invested in a non-profit GTP Artificial Intelligence and created this huge fast-growing investment for what may be considered the new source of the Internet. If this is the case, our future generations may be in harm's way if safety preventions are not legislatively put in place.

Imagine if our President of the United States, or world leaders or government figures or religious leaders are hacked by A.I and it intentionally misleads political citizens, parties, or nations by using misleading information to start wars or society division or even mass genocide.

Some may think that this thought is ridiculous. Why would anyone believe the people we trust to create such a smart tool do so intentionally to be so harmful against humanoids?

Sadly, as a society, what we see and hear with our own eyes and ears, we believe. It also goes along with a reasonable assessment of making sense. Now what's going to happen when these future A.I tool unknowingly even fool the best of us because this computer tool got smarter?

Example: what do our smart phones and computers do when we talk about things that we need?

I cannot tell you how many advertisements of the subject I had inquired about flash across my cell phone and computer, countless advertisements.

What about when an intentional government narratively mandates medical vaccines for people to trust? I have a clear understanding that medical mandates cannot be forced because of our constitutional rights. Sadly, the narrative slowly changes when you question the government mandates you are a subject of misinformation.

The Government medical narrative was that a covid shot would prevent you from getting covid. To get the Jab and you may still catch covid, but it would have been worse if you did not get the Jab.

Regardless of the narrative changing during and post the pandemic, millions died and much evidence was that the Jab had contributed. After the pandemic data, global research was completed by third party expert doctors skeptical of the unproven vaccine in the first place found that the mortality was upon those who had gotten the vaccine shots. Link https://ourworldindata.org

Another example of State Government forced mandates such as NY 2.13 (Google it). In NY, as a public health law, the Court ruling allows the state to Seize Citizens for Indefinite Quarantine and isolation. NY Appeal Court upheld a ruling allowing state officials to detain individuals for public safety reasons, despite concerns about due process violations. This was ruling passed November 22, 2023. If you understand after reading this confused ruling, it basically states that citizens have no rights.

A.I TWO-EDGE Sword for Lairs and Evil Doers

A.I may now unintentionally allow these politicians to use the A.I as an excuse. Blaming the A.I social media aired a statement as A.I false misinformation, although the politician in fact said the criminating statements. How can one really corroborate the truth? If a person who was there as a witness can corroborate truth, the criminal can also produce its false witness.

This type of evil underlining goes back to the beginning in the bible with brothers Cain and Abel. Cain lied about the whereabouts of his slain brother with his statement, "Am I my brother's keeper?" For those with a belief in God's higher power, we know eventually the truth will come forth. Maybe not in this life, but when it counts.

> *As AI technology advances, we must ensure proper regulations to prevent misuse that could lead to societal manipulation and unrest. It's crucial to balance innovation with safeguards to protect future generations.*

A.I Transportation - Elon Musk Tesla owner, entrepreneur, and world influencer.

You may have heard of Elon Musk. You may have heard about this man's futuristic technology vision to reality. Musk, the creator of so many technology expansions such as Telsa vehicles. I have witnessed up close the grand scope of his technology because of the electrical EV power grids being built on my work property of the (LVCVA) Las Vegas Convention and Visitors Authority.

On the LVCVA property, Mr. Musk owns the Boring company who won the bid in 2021 and was hired to build the underground tunnel transportation system that uses Tesla's electric vehicles.

2019 - The Clark County board of directors passed the funding to allow the access underground tunnel to be built from the LVCVA property to the Las Vegas Reed Airport, to Allegiant stadium and underneath the Las Vegas strip. The LVCVA has also purchased the monorail.

2020 - With the LVCVA purchasing the declining above air monorail transportation system, the LVCVA solidified its position, blazing a new trend as sin city's one stop entertainment and business shops. The new perspective as a government run facility it now owns and operates most transportation system in Las Vegas that soon will allow easy access of nonstop direct transportation system from Las Vegas Harry Reed airport, Allegiant Stadium and up and down the Las Vegas Strip Hotels.

This clever planned transformation enthralls the very supports the underling LVCVA brand and mission. Las Vegas is the most desirable destination for both leisure and business travels.

Amazingly, I am witnessing the first electrical grids to power the TESLA computer vehicles. In less than two years, the Tesla electrical grids have already received an updated power boost that allows the EV faster charge in half the time. I can already see a trend of how you can beat this upgrade with a newer upgrade mentality. I am also seeing issues of not enough charging grids and the grids that are being broken into and thieves cutting the copper charging hoses and taking the scrape for money.

As one can note, the future of technology is to create better and faster use of computer-chipped technologies which will change our cultures, our lives, and mindset.

A.I GPT is the new source of technology that has given computers a new brain to revamp everything on wheels. Imagine the 3 million truck drivers who deliver goods and products now replaced by trucks drivers who do not need rest or to be fueled up by gas.

Regardless of what the reality of the battery created materials for these vehicles that are mostly discovered in countries such as China who hate the America way of life because of our abilities to lead the world in technology.

China's threat to dominate the world in technology might find a solution to work with these technology gurus and inventors if the history between China and America is the pattern to deal with these inventors-investors. I expect China will allow nothing vital to pass unless these investors are willing to allow China to invest and control these materials charging an insanely astronomical return that allow their world-leading agenda to be accomplished faster.

The year 2024 brings with it the looming threat of a potential 'EMP' attack using Electric Magnetic Pulse Weapons in the Americas, possibly from China or Russia. Can you imagine our electric advanced technology that depends on electricity knocked out from homes, cars, stores, planes, communications, etc?

Gospel truth is that there must be opposition in all things.

What does this mean? Not all minds are good and think the same when using advanced technology.

Firstly, it takes away the opportunity that people depended on. Secondly, it gives opportunities for criminal hackers and their evil intentions to use such a device or robots to deliver a possible harmful item after hacking without being caught by another human who would act as a safety measure.

Let me share a thought about a piece by a Poet friend titled "Are We?"

Are we a society that has learned from the past and present, are we?

The rights and concepts of our great nation, society and of its people, are we?

Are we learning lessons learned from our forefathers' teachings without concerns, are we?

Are we, yes! We are a better people, a better society, and a better nation.

Let us stand as one, regain lessons learned, and leave no one behind. - ***Alma Franklin***

Generational Gap Philosophy

Dr. Sid Liufau's philosophy, titled GAPCULOGY, explores how modernization is reshaping traditional values and bridging cultural gaps towards the future. The past shapes the future. This way of thinking has its origins in the cultural traditions of previous generations.

However, because of the next generation's cultural changes that are constantly occurring in every generation, which cause generation gaps as a result, which will include A.I technology.

Issues that affect my culture

Past generations of example of my Polynesian Samoan traditional culture have always recognized talking chiefs and high chiefs as the cultural leader who set cultural traditions.

However, from the old generation to the next generation to the latest generation, the changes brought on by wars, religion, environment, disease, drugs have changed cultural generations. I am confident that A.I technology has and will as well.

Chapter 12

MASTERING LISTENING AND LEARNING

Listen to Learn, Then Learn to listen

This statement is also used to listen to what is being narrated and watch the actions of people with agendas. If their actions are the opposite of their words, I would call them liars. Liars are evildoers who have their agenda, which is to bring down America's way of life of freedom, liberty, and justice.

Sadly, the OWO reset is all about taking all the unpaid debts and wiping them out, bringing chaos to the financial structure that is already been passed through executive order and put in place. Reset is a means to implement control over people and invoke new laws that strengthen OWO elites. It does not matter if you are a democrat, republican or independent, the control is for all across the board.

The rest is to affect status, meaning people with no money will still be poor and will be subjected to another set of laws. Reset is to change America's values by implanting a world of change run by AI smart cities that are energy-dependent on these electrical grids, digital cameras, GPS, electric vehicles, smartphones, smart devices, and 5-G towers all over these new smart cities.

Sadly, these smart cities using 5-G towers have already been tested and the multiple 5-G towers themselves have killed birds, and animals and caused cancer among people. These so-called smart cities use social digital platforms.

These people either came here or were born here and raised among the citizens. The evil-doers are even in worldly government leadership positions, military top positions, and high levels of law enforcement.

It is up to you to protect your future with freedom. You can make slight changes such as being engaged and helping future generations, cultures, and people.

Do not allow people outside your culture to change your beliefs through the worldly influences of what they want to change about you and your beliefs. I would rather keep our integrity of cultural civility citizenship with the future generation than lose it to misinformation, misunderstanding, and intentionally corrupt greed.

If you're satisfied with being slaves to whatever you're being told what you must do, then do nothing.

It is this the type of awareness that we would like our future generation to be engaged in, from knowing to questioning to understanding to acting.

What is important is that we as human beings are subjected to keeping the learning and living values of the past, present, and future generations a part of our culture and history.

The most important takeaway is that the past and present generations include the future generation in all dealings, decisions, and results that will affect not just our lives but their lives too.

AI Storm Brewing

In June 2023, I saw a major concern for the Millennials, Gen-Z, and the Alpha generation. You will face a conflict of what I term as (ER) Evidence and Results. However, this acronym for ER is Emergency Response. I tie both Emergency Response and Evidence and Results of this specific futuristic storm brewing out of control for these generations, who are mostly leading the way to being unprepared.

Unprepared because there is no traditional method of resolving issues. Let's say your cell phone, which is your only means of communication, which you totally depend on as your only means of communications to the smart world and the electrical grid goes down indefinitely, what would you do?

Most likely you would respond to what you know, the Millennials, Z-Generation and every future generation from this point forward only know their mode of living communications.

However, for the G-generation and all the past older generations, traditional methods included letter writing, wiretapping, light flash signals, color smoke, even 2-way towerless radios, home connect line phones, pagers and even the early mobile cell phones. Many of these, throughout various generations, were the basic form of communication structure.

So, for those of us who used these means of connecting communications, we could still function in the event that our internet service or cell tower communications electric grid went offline or even knocked out by an EMP charge.

Cyber Attacked and Hacked

In 2023, the United States internet service systems seemed to be the year of failed software protection of data attacks, exposing millions of customers in high-end places. Attacked, such as the mogul corporations of MGM who were hacked and paralyzed to a full stop losing all customer data, Caesars Entertainment was hacked infected and held for ransom in which employees who know shared they paid the hackers, Clorox had to stop production.

Etess Express Freight was hacked. Fed-Ex lost control of a freight plane and had to be emergency landed. Johnson controls building automation contractors that manage countless government buildings.

The Weather Network had its internal Data in the hands of hackers, at least three Connecticut Hospitals, North Carolina Hospitals, New Mexico Insurance Agencies, Sony Entertainment, T-Mobile, a military F-35 Fighter Jet went missing and even NATO was hacked. Imagine all these customers lost affective data, which most likely is being sold on the Black Web for pennies on a dollar.

In 2015, I can recall a discussion I had with one of my daughters who had just graduated in Bio-Medic engineering from Marquette University in Wisconsin. She worked ADA developing A.I prostatic limbs for missing body parts.

I recall I shared with her that if she created an A.I kill-control switch that had the ability to stop all function A.I movements, that she would be an instant billionaire through the dark web.

Why do I say this? I am pretty sure that whatever is being A.I smart chips created for value for a regular citizen or people anywhere in the world that not just our military, but all military forces are considering how to use A.I prostatic limbs to their advantage.

Now consider all these new A.I smart robotic parts, whether on people or on machine parts, and you had the ability to push a button and shut it off or shut it down even after it was put into a smart mode of advancing its defense protection system.

Yes, this sounds like the movie Terminator, Judgment Day, where Skynet controller of all A.I cyber systems. How much would this control switch be valuable to end A.I cyber-attacks worth on humans?

All the recent Artificial Intelligence cyber hacks through these past 10 years and increasing months have shown a clear result and evidence that A.I cyber-protected passwords, data to products are unprotectable.

Now the agenda is to create A.I digital currency, smart vehicles, smart homes, smart tower communications, smart devices, smart robots and smart cities if I were to compare the evidence and results of what our near future A.I forum may look like I would have to place my loyalty to getting rid of Artificial Intelligence as a mean to place our human dependency on as a lost cause of safety and protection.

> ***"The push for AI-driven smart cities and digital currencies threatens our freedoms and traditional values. It's essential to stay vigilant and protect our cultural integrity against these manipulative agendas.***

Artificial Intelligence Gap-Culogy

This intentional A.I system to replace our on-the-spot cash society that allows freedom of access without being monitored is spoken of in the bible, revelation as the prophet John foresaw the future. I am pretty sure many may not know or understand our relationship with technical advance technology A.I smart companies in the US and or other countries that have had the foresight to focus on the need to feel that advanced technology does not mean freedom.

Yes, such advanced technologies make things easier to manage or operate without human beings. However, if AI systems are used, then everyone's ability to have freedom will eventually be compromised.

March 11, 2022, President Joe Biden, unknowingly at the time by others, passed an executive order in America to install A.I digital currency. Which in short means no more access that all currency will be processed through cyber systems.

Headed for a Cashless Society

The simple changes of a cashless society have been going on for years, such as when checking out of food stores to scan your items across the digital scanner, which processes the total amount where you can pay either by credit card or cash. Or at a fast-food restaurant where you access a digital screen, enter your meal items, and pay for it.

What Washington DC has done as a model is that they created the first 15-minute city in whole food stores, which is all AI runs. It is implemented on a digital passport which you must check in, used to check out supplies, check out of stores and the digital passport is based on your digital credit scores. If your digital credit scores are too low, then there is no supply for you.

As a matter of fact, if one has a poor digital social score, it may or could translate to no food, no water, no gas, no flights, no provisions. Whole Foods stores are the first 15-minute cities being created to lead the way into AI supplies' future.

This insight points to the way to keep control of the people by ushering in a preventive way. If you help others who have poor digital social credit scores, then you may be complicit in circumventing the system and added to being locked out.

Consider the reason the evildoers have allowed illegals to bypass the borders and give them access to the government's future run system.

Consider the A.I system to be intended for the world change. Many people who want change and hate America came here and now have access to digital currency and can start a new life or return home and have the new AI system that will be implemented throughout the world.

The A.I Future is Already Now

Citizen entrepreneurs have gone into the Uber driving business. In which they use their personal vehicles to pick up food orders and transport the food orders to the customer. This is a business and yes, they get paid using a software app for ordering meals.

Unlike the usual 9-5 job, this particular type of employment provided a much-needed breath of fresh air. This allowed the entrepreneurs the freedom to work their own schedules whenever they wanted, not having to commit on a regular schedule and be ridiculed by overshadowing supervisors.

Equipped with a dependable vehicle, insurance, cell phone or laptop and a GPS device is all that was required.

Now let's welcome the competition, the A. I smart robots that indeed exist and have been designed to deliver food to a customer without a human from a local fast-food restaurant or supply stores to the customers.

And whoever can afford these high-end expensive Robot transportation devices will seem to have the advantage of not having to worry about depending on other humans, benefits, and or insurance. Therefore, finding new ways to expand their financial means and profits.

Sadly, these types of advanced technology also currently serve a two-fold safety issue.

- The danger of this advanced technology is that it will replace human beings who are currently depending on this financial means to make a living. It is easier to self-generate and sustain cost-wise the data is still out.

- Consider if the evil design and intention to deliver something harmful without putting themselves in harm's way.

Digital Currency is the future of AI seemingly it will require all people to eventually pay with a digital payment passport. To shop in AI stores, attend city events, ride government transportation, even private transportation, and get electrical power, seemingly only the government will be the ones to issue anything through a digital passport.

Consider the past and present opportunities we could work under the table for extra money. This Digital currency puts a stop to it all. No more currency can be offered without the government having a say.

The takeaway is that the Government uses AI systems for managing and controlling.

Let those who have wisdom understand. When you give up something, it is replaced by something else.

The Bible Revelations 13: 15-18

15 *And he had power to give life unto the image of the beast, that the image of the beast should both speak, and cause that as many as would not worship the image of the beast should be killed.*

16 *And he causeth all, both small and great, rich and poor, free and bond, to receive a mark in their right hand, or in their foreheads:*

17 *And that no man might buy or sell, save he that had the mark, or the name of the beast, or the number of his name.*

***18** Here is wisdom. So let him that hath understanding count the number of the beast: for it is the number of a man; and his number is Six hundred threescore and six.*

This passage sums it up to you to recognize things all around us that eventually will go astray, and we will have to make our choices about where we will stand. As for me and my household, I will serve the Lord God almighty.

My Perspective and what I have come to know

- The important thing is to not give away your freedom, your rights, or your voice.

- Why care about having to walk until you cannot walk anymore because of an accident or illness?

Chapter 13

CULTURAL AND GENERATIONAL CHANGE FEELINGS

The same profound feelings lie with culture changes and future generational changes.

A generation that has never had this type of experience of not having freedom being overseen by governance through government laws and policies may indeed give control to the governance's voice for the human future.

The voices of governance may sound reasonable, yet they do not understand the importance of losing one's freedom from governance instruction since they have never experienced freedom before.

Once freedom is gone and governance is controlled through force or coercion, it is almost impossible for that generation to break free, as the propaganda of lies and misinformation will have the very people you trust turn against you. If you fight against the governance voice of information, this is what Hitler did to the German people. He used the method of divide and conquer through national pride for the love of country and government.

If you plotted against national politics, you would be considered an enemy to the nation and its government all in the name of safety.

15-minute Smart city agendas are a One-world government system being instituted by the world's elite 1% billionaires and trillionaires who have companies like BlackRock and Vanguard, an investment mogul who has purchased 60% of the homes in the United States.

They have unleashed a plan titled the Great Reset, which is to buy and control most of the housing, land, farms, A.I platform, private security forces, 5G towers, yes even space force (DEW) Direct Energy Weapon, etc.

Everything and anything that prepares to record all individual movements, sounds and I will go even as far as the day will come if not prevented even intentions will be predetermined as guilt by overseeing big brother who does not like, agree, support anything that stands against their agenda which is absolutely an attack on one's constitutional rights.

I am not saying we do have to stop A.I completely. I am saying it should be used in certain venues of limited capacity. To create a total A.I electrical grid as a smart city is absolutely a bad choice that will hurt human beings.

CONCLUSION

Embracing Change, Fostering Peace

In our final analysis of "Gapculogy," it is apparent that the intersections of tradition and modernity are not merely sites of discord but also offer great potential for development and fostering understanding. Throughout this book, we've explored the dynamic processes by which cultural gaps are created and bridged, highlighting the crucial role of modernization in reshaping our traditional values. We've seen how these shifts impact generational divides, race relations, business practices, religious beliefs, and intercultural communications. The insights garnered from these discussions serve not only as reflections on our current state but also as forces guiding us toward a more inclusive and peaceful future.

Key Insights and Lessons

1. Adaptation is inevitable: Cultural evolution is an ongoing process. Embracing change rather than resisting it allows us to adapt more effectively and collectively.

2. Education is crucial: Promoting an understanding of cultural shifts through education can significantly mitigate conflicts and misunderstandings.

3. Civility as a Foundation: Maintaining civility is essential in our interactions, ensuring that even amidst disagreement, respect, and peace are preserved.

Calls to Action

1. For Individuals: Remain open and curious. Engage with different cultures, ask questions, and listen sincerely. Foster environments where diverse voices are not only heard but also valued.

2. For Communities: Create platforms for dialogue and exchange. Support community-led initiatives that celebrate cultural diversity and promote inclusivity.

3. For Policymakers: Implement policies that recognize and protect cultural identities while promoting social cohesion. Ensure that laws and regulations adapt to the changing cultural landscapes to remain relevant and supportive of all community members.

The Ongoing Journey of Cultural Adaptation and Peace-Building:

The journey towards fully bridging cultural gaps is continuous and requires commitment from each one of us. As we look to the future, we must carry forward the lessons of Gapculogy, applying them to new challenges and opportunities. Building a peaceful society in the face of cultural evolution is not only about adapting to changes but also about actively shaping these changes to foster a community that upholds the dignity and worth of every individual.

In closing, the takeaway for Gapculogy is founded on the construct of Truth. If we deny or destroy our history, culture, and or deny recognized contributions to the cultural stories, or our upbringing, ways of life, or even others who have contributed to the whole of progression.

Let us then compare President Lincoln's quote; "It is the reason that we may give a limb to save a life, but never a life to save a limb.

In the film "Monument Men", Actor George Cloony delivers a line that rings true in support of humanitarian cores.

As protectors of humanitarian identity and cultural history, we must preserve cultural art, paintings, monuments, tapestries, jewelry, tattoos, or any achievements that perpetuate and fashion one's cultural history and way of life.

Sadly, a generation of people can be wiped out. You can burn their homes down and run them off their lands however, somehow, they will come back around.

But if you destroy their culture, history, and achievements, then it's like it never happened, just like ash floating in the air and that is what evil wants, no hope for perpetuating culture and history.

The quote 'out of sight out of mind.' We do not have to agree, or even support the evil and bad things that occurred in the past that perpetuate evil, however, reminders of human histories whether good or bad are a necessity.

Anyone who is bent on forcing others to destroy past cultures, histories, shrines, monuments, art, paintings, tapestries, tattoos, and jewelry, even if they remind us of evil people, places, or history.

The thought of getting rid of these reminders of humanity's crimes so they cannot remind us of our past is wrong. 'If we do not learn from our history's past, then we may be doomed to repeat itself.'

Translated, it's the stories of our lives or histories translated onto any of these venues that recognize cultural way of life. It will be with every breath I take I will fight to stand up for the truth both that are good and bad so that it may remain as a reminder of our humanity's history.

I pray our perspectives may be as joyful as this quote. "Life is a Luau". May we feast and enjoy the educational and experiential truths that have resulted from the good, bad, and ugly?

If you're not happy with the results of life's current situation, then change your views with ones that ring true and bring you happiness.

In embracing change and fostering peace, we affirm our collective responsibility to not just coexist, but to thrive together in a world marked by incredible diversity and rapid transformation. Let us move forward with hope and determination, committed to the ongoing work of crafting a world where cultural gaps are bridged with understanding and respect.

As we close this book, let us open our minds and hearts to the endless possibilities that lie in our ability to adapt and grow together.

ABOUT THE AUTHOR

Dr. Sid Liufau, MTC, HCC, CIT, is the Co-founder of the Civility For All Foundation (CFAF), a non-profit organization dedicated to consulting, educating, training, and resolving issues related to disagreements to mental health care philosophies and solutions for all individuals.

Born on November 22nd, 1963, in Kahuku, Oahu, Dr. Liufau's life journey has shaped his commitment to promoting civility and addressing mental health challenges in society.

In the 1970s, Dr. Liufau's family relocated from Oahu to Orange County, California, where he grew up alongside his siblings. Despite the challenges stemming from his biological father's infidelity, Dr. Liufau admired his mother's strength and resilience. His mother later remarried, and Dr. Liufau's stepfather became a positive influence in his life, raising him and his siblings as his own.

During his formative years from 1975 to 1985, Dr. Liufau embraced his Polynesian heritage while immersing himself in modern American culture. He attended junior high, high school, and Fullerton College in Orange County, where he excelled in various fields, such as theatrical art and minor criminal justice. Additionally, he delved into the realm of self-defense, learning the skills of Lima Lama and studying Kenpo karate under esteemed masters.

In 1984, Dr. Liufau's passion for his Samoan fire-knife culture and drumming led him to a successful decade-long career in entertainment at Disneyland and Walt Disney World. His dedication, abilities, and humility allowed him to thrive in the entertainment industry.

From 1989 to 1991, Dr. Liufau undertook a Labor of Love Mission in Chicago, Illinois, driven by his faith and a desire to help others. This experience further instilled in him the importance of Christ-like principles and the fulfillment that comes from selfless service.

Following his mission, Dr. Liufau pursued stunt work as Batman at Great America, eventually transitioning to a full-time film and television career in Los Angeles. Throughout his professional endeavors, he balanced his personal life, and in 2001, he married Sharene Teruya. They have since been blessed with five children and seven grandchildren, bringing joy and fulfillment to their family life.

In 2004, Dr. Liufau took a hiatus from the entertainment industry and secured full-time employment as a county convention authority officer. Simultaneously, he established his family business, 'Poly-wood Entertainment,' which showcased a Polynesian dance production and dinner show called "Island Heat" at the Treasure Island Hotel in Las Vegas.

In 2018, Dr. Liufau's life took a transformative turn when he attended a community leadership meeting on Asian hate crimes. Dr. Liufau enrolled in Dr. Rivers' training on anti-hate mongering after hearing Dr. Rivers' message of civility and solutions. Recognizing the impact of mental health challenges on his children, who were dealing with anxiety, stress, and depression, Dr. Liufau committed himself to learning and promoting civility to address these issues.

The COVID-19 pandemic in 2020 brought significant challenges to Dr. Liufau's community and professional life. Furloughed from his job along with many others, he redirected his focus towards learning and helping those in need within the Asia Pacific Islander community. He witnessed the adverse effects of the pandemic, particularly on mental health, especially among the youth who faced school closures and isolation.

In recognition of his contributions and commitment to promoting civility, Dr. Liufau was awarded an Honorary Doctorate on September 11, 2022, by Dr. Clyde Rivers and Dr. Robin Lococo of the International Civility Network (ICN). This acknowledgment solidified his position as a global leader in civility philosophy and solution platforms. Together with Dr. Rozita Lee, Dr. Elvira, and Advisor Vincent Souza, Dr. Liufau established the Civility For All Foundation, a nonprofit organization that currently focuses on training individuals in mental health care philosophies and solutions centered on civility.

Today, Dr. Sid Liufau continues to prioritize the well-being of his family, employment, community service, and sharing his personal testimony of finding happiness through faith in Jesus Christ. He remains committed to promoting civility and addressing mental health chal-lenges, aiming to create a more compassionate and understanding society.

THE CIVILITY FOR ALL FOUNDATION (CFAF)

The Civility For All Foundation (CFAF) is a nonprofit organization dedicated to promoting communication health and resolving issues related to mental health care philosophies and solutions for all individuals. The International Civility Network, I Change Nations (ICN), and its World Civility Ambassador, HRH Dr. Clyde Rivers, support the foundation that Dr. Sid Liufau and Dr. Rozita Lee, HCC, founded.

The primary mission of CFAF is to consult, educate, train, and provide resources to address communication issues and promote awareness of civility in all communities, both locally and globally. The foundation recognizes the negative impact of division, conflict, hostility, anger, and hate crimes resulting from a lack of understanding and effective communication.

CFAF offers a range of classes and courses to foster civility, including Civility Fundamentals, Civility Gap Generations, Civility Gap-culogy, and Civility Communication Health. These classes and courses, overseen by Dr. Sid Liufau and Dr. Rozita Lee, aim to bridge the communication gap and promote harmonious relationships within diverse communities, and these programs are also designed to equip individuals with the tools and knowledge to foster positive communication and bridge gaps between different groups.

The Foundation is actively working on developing online sessions and internet-based resources to make its programs accessible to a broader audience. By focusing on communication health, CFAF aims to create safe spaces for dialogue and understanding, ultimately contributing to peaceful interactions within society.

The World Medical Organization has recognized CFAF as a legitimate humanitarian health service falling under the Humanitarian Civility Council (HCC). The Canadian Health and Humanitarian Organization also acknowledges the organization. These recognitions highlight the importance of communication health and its impact on overall well-being and harmonious coexistence.

The Foundation operates according to bylaws and has an elected board of members and chair committees that adhere to moral, ethical, and principled codes of conduct. Their commitment to these standards ensures that the foundation's work aligns with its mission and goals.

Through their initiatives, CFAF aims to contribute to resolving mental health issues and promoting civility across various communities. By providing consultations, education, training, and resources, the organization strives to foster understanding, empathy, and respectful communication, ultimately creating a more harmonious and inclusive society for all.

Internally and externally, CFAF plans to offer student classes, course sessions, and virtual sessions in the future. By providing accessible education and training, the organization aims to empower individuals and communities to address communication issues effectively.

CFAF is committed to upholding moral, ethical, and principled codes of conduct. The organization's bylaws and elected board members ensure its operations align with these values, promoting integrity and accountability in all endeavors.

In summary, the Civility For All Foundation (CFAF) is a nonprofit organization dedicated to promoting communication health and resolving issues of division, conflict, and hate crimes. Through consultation, education, training, and providing solutions, CFAF aims to create a more harmonious and understanding society for all.